How to Fly for Free

Linda Bowman

PROBUS PUBLISHING COMPANY
Chicago, Illinois

Library of Congress Cataloging in Publication Data Available.

ISBN   1-55738-217-4

Printed in the United States of America

BB

1   2   3   4   5   6   7   8   9   0

TABLE OF CONTENTS

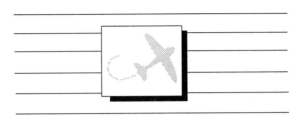

CHAPTER 3
FLYING FOR FREE
59

INTRODUCTION

INTRODUCTION

"I'm sorry sir, but you don't qualify for any of those low fares that you read about."

"That's right, because you are not staying over Saturday night, your fare increases from $189 to $1,000."

"To get the best fare, you will have to make three stops, which will add almost six hours onto your flying time."

"I'm sorry, you can't get your money back even though you have to cancel that flight."

How often have we heard statements like these from the airlines and our travel agents? Of course, they are said with such authority that we end up believing them.

Yet, by accident several years ago, I discovered we are being severely misled by almost all of those "voices of authority" in the travel industry. After some investigation, I learned that there are many perfectly legal ways to get great bargains on air travel *by taking advantage of the airlines' own rules and regulations.* By using a little creativity, substantial savings are very easy to achieve.

The big problem, however, is *finding* out about these special fares and money-saving situations such as:

- Charter flight fares
- Hidden-city fares
- Discount tickets sold by consolidators
- Off-peak fares
- High/low season fares
- Using coupons from frequent flyer awards
- Bump coupons
- Passes for unlimited or multi-trip travel
- Senior discounts
- Last minute or emergency travel
- Group discounts
- Corporate discounts
- Group and children's discounts
- Travel clubs

The airlines won't tell you. Honestly, when was the last time an airline agent said, "Let me spend some time trying to work out the best possible fare for you."? Your travel agent, although well intentioned, usually can't spend the time and often doesn't have the information available to search out the best fares for you. Yet, there are tons of ways to fly for free or at substantial savings.

I discovered the airfare "cover up" by accident when I booked a round-trip flight from Los Angeles to Chicago. I had seen advertisements for tickets ranging from $198 round trip to $298. However, when I called the airline to make my reservations, I was told by the airlines clerk that "You must not have read the *fine print*. You have to stay over a Saturday night; you have to make your reservations 30 days in advance; you have to pay for your ticket within 48 hours; you must complete your travel by...".

Hearing all this, I accepted her explanation and asked for the next best fare (which I expected to be between $400 and $500). I was shocked when she told me that the only other fare I could qualify for was over $1,000! But, if I could stay over a Saturday night, which would not only ruin my weekend, but cost hundreds of dollars more in extra hotel bills, food, and other expenses, I could take advantage of a lower "special" fare.

That's when I discovered a method that not only allowed me to fly to Chicago round-trip, nonstop for almost one half the "best" quote from the airlines, but also provided me with another free round-trip ticket to Chicago, allowing me to make another business stop that I needed to make on the way. (Also free.)

This meant that my second flight to Chicago was, in fact, better than free because, whereas the cheapest fare for my original business trip was $1,060, I was able to have two separate trips for under $700, in effect I was being paid $400 to take another trip that I needed to take anyway. (See Chapter 5 for what I would have done if I didn't need to take this second trip.)

Was this a hypothetical, once-in-a-lifetime deal that couldn't be duplicated again? No. It's an easy-to-use method that not only worked then, but one that has been used many times since by myself, my friends, and business associates.

Further, I learned that it is not necessary to be bound by the restrictions found in tiny print at the bottom of those giant full-page newspaper ads. I have almost always been able to change my departure date or time to meet my convenience, even though the ticket specifically prohibited my doing so, even though the airline agents say you can't do it. (Recently, I used this procedure to get a group of 10 home earlier than our *nonrefundable, nonchangeable* tickets allowed.)

Knowing these methods of air travel has allowed my family and our friends to take trips that we never thought we could afford and still fly with the convenience and freedom that we thought were available only to the big spenders. (My family and I just returned from a two-week skiing trip in Switzerland and Austria flying nonstop on the best airlines, and staying at deluxe resorts for the same price it would have cost us to take an average ski vacation in the United States. It was the trip of a lifetime for my family, affordable only by using the methods we'll talk about in this book.)

Believe it or not, this is only the tip of the iceberg. As I looked further, I saw so many unheard of, unbelievable ways to save time and money flying that it amazed me. However, these opportunities are almost unknown or undisclosed by the airlines and therefore overlooked by 99 percent of travelers. Even if you only make one trip every year or two, the savings can be substantial enough to allow a family to take a vacation they thought they could never afford (as we did with our European ski vacation).

This book will focus on the topics that are so important to most travelers—concrete ways of getting the best deal, that everyone can use. It is an easy to understand, hands-on guide that easily takes you around the fine print and misleading information on air travel. We will give you the specific methods, (including the names and phone numbers of the best companies and sources that we have found) that will allow you to fly for free, or at least as cheaply as possible.

CHAPTER
1
GETTING STARTED:
EXPLAINING THE BASICS

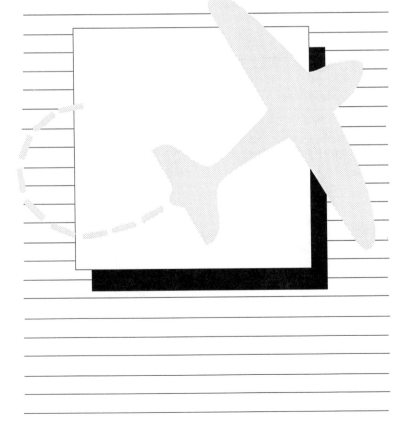

GETTING STARTED: EXPLAINING THE BASICS

WHERE DO I BEGIN?

There are three ways to make airline travel arrangements:

1. Through a travel agent.
2. By calling the airlines servicing your destination.
3. By doing the legwork, research and comparisons yourself and having the travel agent make the final reservations and do the ticketing.

All three ways have their benefits and problems.

Any airline you call is going to, naturally, try to get you to fly with them claiming to have best service, cheapest fares, most flights, etc. While they may not purposely "lie" to you, the information they give is often incomplete, "half-truths" that are, at best, misleading. For example: airlines can quote you fares for "direct" flights which many people assume to be nonstop. They are not. "Direct" means only no change of planes. But there can be several stops at other airports along the way.

On the other hand, if you are a regular customer, some travel agents may be willing to do the research to get the lowest possible fare. However, they may not have all the computerized information available to them, since there are three major airline computer reservation systems and most travel agents use only one.

Also, these systems are owned by airlines such as American, TWA, and United, so the lowest fare on a nonsponsoring airline may be unavailable to them. Most agents just do not have the time, information, or knowledge to research the best fares for your trip.

If you have a good relationship with a local travel agent, he or she may actually appreciate you doing the time-consuming leg-work and coming back to the travel agency to confirm your plans (and prices), issue the tickets, and even deliver them to you. That way the agent still makes a commission even though you've done most of the work. Also included in the "travel agent" category are automobile clubs, gasoline companies, and credit card companies that offer travel services.

One of the most frequent recent complaints by travel agents is the rise in the number of "shopping around" calls they receive from anonymous travelers they never hear from again. So, if you are planning to use a travel agency, find a good one and stick with them. Be loyal and give them your business regularly. Unless the call is from a good customer, a typical agent has no incentive to make a time-consuming, thorough air-fare comparison. However, agents can and will be extremely diligent to loyal, repeat customers.

However, as we mentioned, even good agents are limited to the information in their computers. Most of them are not familiar with many of the methods we present in our book. Smaller airlines and ever-changing promotions abound, so that even the most diligent agent has a hard time keeping up to speed.

WHAT DO I DO NEXT?

Begin by calling several airlines and your travel agent (we are going to assume you have been able to select a knowledgeable one you like) to find out which airlines have the best price to your destination and ask them the following:

What is the cheapest fare for coach/economy service?

What restrictions are there such as: advance purchase, weekday travel, minimum stay, cancellation penalty, limited seats, and is there one or more stops or a connection?

If you can't meet some or all of the requirements, then ask:

What is the lowest fare for a nonstop flight?

What's the lowest price for a flight not requiring minimum stay?

What's the best price for a flight leaving in less than a week's time or sooner?

What is the cheapest fare if you have to travel one or both ways on a weekend?

These basic questions will get you rolling; you can then explore other special fares. (We'll cover all this good stuff later.)

BEING AN INFORMED FLYER

If you travel frequently or have the time and desire to really keep abreast of the various and constantly changing air fares and routes, then you might:

- Keep a file of the cheap flight advertisements from the Sunday travel section of a large metropolitan newspaper in your area.

- Subscribe to travel magazines, periodicals, flight guides (the *Official Airline Guide*, *OAG*, is the most complete and universally subscribed to).

- Check the classified ads of the daily and Sunday newspaper for other "undiscovered" fares and deals.

- Compare the latest super low "limited time only" promotional fares offered by competing airlines.

Below are listed air travel periodicals and their phone numbers and the three monthly pocket flight guides that cover North American air travel:

PERIODICALS AND NEWSLETTERS

Publication	Telephone Number
Airline Passenger Service	(213) 493-4877
Best Fares — The USA Report	(800) 635-3033
Business Travelers International (focuses on European Travel)	(212) 697-1700
Consumer Reports Travel Letter	(800) 525-0643
Corporate Travel Magazine	(800) 223-6767
Executive Travel	(212) 867-2080
Family Travel Times	(212) 206-0688
Frequent	(719) 597-8889
Frequent Flyer	(800) 323-3537
International Living	(301) 234-0515
Nationwide Intelligence Briefings	(617) 229-5853
Partners in Travel	(213) 476-4869
Runzheimer Reports	(708) 291-9011
Side Streets of the World	(212) 431-1652
Travel Management Daily	(212) 977-8312
Travelore Report	(215) 735-3838
Travel Smart	(800) FARE-OFF
Traveler's Advisory	(800) 222-9477

Three publications we especially like are *Best Fares —The USA Report, Travel Smart,* and *Consumer Reports Travel Letter.*

Best Fares is a monthly bulletin giving briefs on the latest travel promotions for airlines, hotel chains, car rental agencies, frequent flyers, seniors, and business and leisure discounts. There are also listings of important phone numbers and contacts in the travel industry. Each issue includes several pages of inexpensive fares to major cities around the country and a very thorough section listing "Hidden City" fares for traveling to major "hub" destinations via less expensive cities.

Travel Smart is a monthly newsletter covering the latest promotions, deals, and specials in all areas of travel. They also have book and catalog listings, cruise schedules, travel tips, and developments in the industry worth noting. *Consumer Reports Travel Letter* is also a very thorough monthly newsletter that reports on all aspects of consumer travel including in-depth reports in specific areas and changes in government regulations and laws affecting consumer travel. It also includes, for reference, an index of past reports, which can be ordered individually through *CRTL.*

Frequent and *Frequent Flyer* are publications aimed for the business flyer, focusing on the latest changes and additions to the airlines' frequent flier programs.

MONTHLY POCKET FLIGHT GUIDES

Guide	Telephone Number
American Express Sky Guide	(800) 678-6738
Executive Flight Planner	(617) 262-5000
OAG Pocket Flight Guide	(800) 323-3537

These publications list all the scheduled nonstop and direct flights, some connecting flights, times of departure and arrival, type of plane, what meals are served, and how much time you need to catch connecting flights at the airport. They are very helpful in mapping out all of the possible connections and alternative routes for a trip you are planning.

You can also join travel clubs and read the literature and information they send on a regular basis. If you're really serious about tracking all available information, subscribe to one or more of the computerized flight schedules which can be accessed by a home computer. These systems include:

COMPUTERIZED FLIGHT SCHEDULE SERVICES

Schedule	Telephone Number
ABC Worldwide Hotel and Travel Guide	(617) 262-5000
OAG Electronic Edition	(800) 323-3537
TWA Travelshopper	(800) 892-1011

Keep an up-to-date file of the special airline promotional fares usually advertised in the weekday editions of newspapers. File them under expiration date, so you can make use of them while they are valid, then toss them once they've expired.

Keeping track of all these research materials and advertising will assure you a good deal in your future air travel. Granted, it will cost you time, but if you are looking for the absolutely lowest cost in getting where you want to go by air, then making a serious effort will pay off. Doing this and applying it with the other methods described in the rest of this book will give you the knowledge and ability to be a savvy, smart, money-saving traveler.

Finally, being an informed flyer also means keeping up with major changes in the airline industry that directly affect individual travelers. Specifically, in the past two years, two major airlines, Braniff and Eastern, have shut down and several others are operating under the protection of federal bankruptcy laws. Among them: Pan Am, once the flagship airline of the United States overseas; Continental, which had absorbed Texas International, Midway, New York Air, Frontier and People's Express. Others have defaulted on debt payments or laid off tens of thousands of workers due to the deteriorating financial conditions of the airline industry. A recent (April, 1991) Associated Press article stated that "of 17 new airlines formed between 1979 and 1985, 14 no longer fly. . . . Still, observers predict the skies may soon be thinned even further. Among those named as probable survivors: United, American and Delta. Northwest says it should be added to the list."

What does all this mean to individual travelers? We suggest your best protection from loss in these situations is paying for all your airline tickets with a credit card that can be voided later. Tickets paid for by cash or check may not be refundable. Also, travelers with significant frequent flyer mileage on any airline should use up their mileage if the carrier goes out of business.

CHAPTER
2
DISCOUNT FARES

DISCOUNT FARES

Most people know only about "regular" full fares or the "cheap" fares they see advertised in the newspapers. Many other discount fares go undiscovered by average travelers who are under the misconception that the heavily discounted fares they see advertised in the newspaper will not apply to them. They are concerned about being required to fly at inconvenient times, making many stopovers, or other complications and difficulties. While it is true that the many fares, requirements, and restrictions make it confusing, difficult, and time-consuming to plan an economical trip, in this section we will show you how to remove these roadblocks.

Several kinds of discount fares are available that provide savings off the nonrestricted coach/economy fare for a regularly scheduled flight published by an airline. They include restricted/special fares, Apex, MaxSaver, excursion, or "limited capacity." Fitting the restrictions of the lowest published fare, the excursion, MaxSaver (domestic), or Apex (international) fare, is the easiest way to get a discount. This can save you an average of 60 percent off the full coach fare. The restrictions usually require:

- Purchase of your ticket in advance.

- Stay a minimum number of days including a weekend night.

- A cancellation penalty.

- A nonrefundable restriction (partial or completely nonrefundable).
- A connection or one or more stops.

If you can't meet all the restrictions, see which ones you *do* meet. Often there are special fares available for each separate requirement. For example, you may be willing to make one or two extra stops to save money instead of time. Also, keep checking the availability of the excursion/Apex fares as your flight date nears. The flight may be only partially booked, and either more cheap seats will become available (if they were sold out earlier) or the airline may waive the restrictions for new purchases at the lower fare. Since airlines can lower the fare to whatever it takes to get passengers to fly, they will always make more of a profit on a filled seat sold at a discount than on an empty seat not sold at all.

For the same reason, we have always been able to change our "nonchangeable" restricted reservation to an earlier flight that is either more convenient to us or may be a better flight. This is done by presenting our ticket to the agent at the gate, who places us on a "stand-by" basis. This allows us a seat on any flight that is not completely booked 10 minutes prior to departure.

We were going to include actual recent examples of advertisements describing some of the most popular discount programs that are available at different times during the year. As we mentioned already, knowledge of these fares and programs can save you up to 80 percent off of full fare tickets; but the problem is finding out about these fares and their availability. If you call to make reservations, it is doubtful that the airline reservation clerk or even your own travel agent will be aware of all the current money-saving options.

However, when we contacted most of the major airlines for permission to run their ads, they refused. A few of them expressed what we feel was the real reason for turning down our request—if "everyone" knew about these money saving fares It could cost them millions of dollars—especially from travelers who would have paid full fare anyway.

OFF-PEAK TIMES

Another way to save money off the full fare is to fly at nonpeak travel times. It makes sense that flying would be cheaper when fewer people are flying and there is an abundance of empty seats. Off-peak times include flying at night (especially late at night) and on holidays, such as Thanksgiving, Christmas, and New Year's. For example, airlines once refused to advertise discount holiday fares until the last minute. But they are now promoting far in advance "Kringle" fares that cut prices by as much as 70 percent for travel to most U.S. locations on December 24, 25, 29, 30, and 31, and January 4, 5, and 6.

OFF-PEAK SEASON AND
HIGH-LOW SEASON TRAVEL

To boost revenue during off-peak seasons, airlines often offer reduced fares in one or more of their classes (economy, coach, etc.). They usually carry restrictions (direction of travel, day of week, minimum and maximum stay, advance purchase, limited seats, nonrefundable) since they are "special" fares. Nevertheless, they can be significantly cheaper than full, nonrestricted fares. If you want to go to a ski resort area during the summer, when it is less popular, book your flights from April through the summer months up through Thanksgiving.

The reverse holds true as well. Summer resorts, which are most popular from June to August, will be more economical from September to mid-December. Some of the very hot desert destinations like Las Vegas, Palm Springs, and Arizona (considered winter vacation destinations) are often cheaper to visit during their steamy off-season months of mid-June, July, and August.

Traveling on international routes can also offer some cost-saving opportunities. These routes, linking the United States with Asia, Europe, South America, and the South Pacific, have at least two seasonal price levels. The price levels are referred to as high (H) and low (L) and are limited to economy excursion fares. Some routes have only one high and one low season each year; others may have several ups and downs. And there are the times in between the high and low seasons that are called "shoulder" seasons. There are also separate price levels for these times.

In most instances, the round-trip fare you pay is determined by the date on which you start your travel. The North American routes such as those described above for ski and sun resorts are generally *not* designated as seasonal. However, with deregulation, the airlines change fares as often as they wish. Thus, in reality they make what amounts to seasonal adjustments without labeling them as such. Sometimes they will designate "blackout" times during holiday and high demand periods.

On the following page is a sampling of high, low, and shoulder seasons for travel in Europe, Eastern Europe and destinations in the Orient.

LESS POPULAR DESTINATION TRAVEL

If you are flying to a major metropolitan area or a very popular destination, it is often cheaper to fly into a nearby airport that is less popular. You can use ground transportation to get to your final destination. For example, instead of flying into San Francisco, you may want to choose Oakland or San Jose. Instead of Los Angeles, fly to San Diego. Or avoid the crowds and confusion of Chicago's O'Hare Airport by flying to Milwaukee's Mitchell International. Whether you rent a car and drive yourself or take public transportation (train or bus), the extra time you spend on the road seeing the countryside can be more relaxing than the time spent waiting for your luggage to arrive, sitting on crowded runways, or circling a too busy airport. You may even arrive

EUROPE

Eastbound:
LO: Nov. 1 - Dec. 14, 1990
SH: Dec. 15 - Dec. 24, 1990
LO: Dec. 25 - Mar. 31, 1990
SH: Apr. 1 - June 14, 1991
HI: June 15 - Sept. 15, 1991
SH: Sept. 16 - Oct. 31, 1991
LO: Nov. 1 - Dec. 12, 1991
SH: Dec. 13 - Dec. 24, 1991
LO: Dec. 25 - Mar. 31, 1992

Westbound:
LO: Nov. 1 - Dec. 27, 1990
SH: Dec. 28 - Jan. 6, 1991
LO: Jan. 7 - Mar. 31, 1991
SH: Apr. 1 - June 14, 1991
HI: June 15 - Sept. 30, 1991
SH: Oct.1 - Oct. 31, 1991
LO: Nov. 1 - Dec. 26, 1991
SH: Dec. 27 - Jan. 5, 1992
LO: Jan. 6 - Mar. 31, 1992

EASTERN EUROPE

Eastbound:

LO: Nov. 1, 1990 - Apr. 15, 1991
SH: Apr. 16 - May 31, 1991
HI: June 1 - July 20, 1991
SH: July 21 - Oct. 31, 1991
LO: Nov. 1 - Dec. 12, 1991
SH: Dec. 13 - Dec. 25, 1991
LO: Dec. 26 - Dec. 31, 1991

Westbound:
LO: Nov. 1 - Apr. 15, 1991
SH: Apr. 15 - Aug. 14, 1991
HI: Aug. 15 - Sept. 14, 1991
SH: Sept. 15 - Oct. 31, 1991
LO: Nov. 1 - Dec. 12, 1991
SH: Dec. 13 - Dec. 25, 1991
LO: Dec. 26 - Dec. 31, 1991

TOKYO

LO: Nov. 1, 1990 - Mar. 31, 1991
SH: Apr. 1 - May 31, 1991
HI: June 1 - Aug. 31, 1991
SH: Sept. 1 - Oct. 31, 1991
LO: Nov. 1 - Dec. 14, 1991

BALI

Year round rates apply from Nov. 1,
1990 - Dec. 14, 1991

MANILA

LO: Nov. 1 - Nov. 30, 1990
HI: Dec. 1 - Dec. 31, 1990
LO: Jan. 1 - May 31, 1991
HI: June 1 - June 30, 1991
SH: July 1 - Aug. 31, 1991
LO: Sept. 1 - Nov. 30, 1991

earlier, considering the kinds of problems and hassles that are likely at the "big city" airports.

Another reason for flying to and from secondary airports is that flyers typically end up paying more when traveling from airports dominated by a single airline. A recent study by the Tucson Airport Authority concluded that fares at larger airports are from 10 to 34 percent higher than at medium-sized airports that are located nearby. The lack of competition at these "hub" airports discourages the usual price-slashing wars that are more common at medium-sized hubs with a greater number of smaller airlines competing for passengers.

If you don't want to go to the nearby airport, but you also don't want to pay the high fares of the only airline flying directly to your destination, break the trip up using two competing airlines with a plane change in the middle. This is known as "interlining," and if your goal is practicality, this is one way to go. For example, at one time the unrestricted one-way fare from Dallas to Nashville was $355 on American and Delta. However, flying to Houston on American, Continental, or Delta and connecting to American or Southwest to Nashville costs $155, saving $200 or over *50 percent.*

COMPANION FARES

Companion fares are "back door" discount fares that have enjoyed renewed popularity in recent years especially with uncertain economic conditions and rising fuel prices causing passengers to think twice before taking along a spouse (or "significant other"). A companion fare can be either a free ticket or an inexpensive fixed-fare ticket that is offered in conjunction with the purchase of an excursion or economy fare round-trip ticket. Some examples of companion fares include:

- Continental offered a free round trip companion fare when purchased with a MaxSaver round-trip ticket to over 130 destinations in the continental United States. This promotion, was followed by nearly every major U.S. airline, offering similar free companion tickets with round-trip MaxSaver fares to most destinations within the United States.

- Continental also recently offered a free companion ticket for family members of business class and first class passengers taking international flights originating in the mainland United States.

- Southwest Airlines introduced a $20 companion fare in a cosponsored promotion with American Express. Passengers needed to purchase tickets with an American Express card at least one day in advance of travel. Competing airlines America West and United Airlines matched Southwest's companion fare in selected competing markets.

- Air France offered a "Buy One, Get One Free" companion ticket for flights on its newly introduced routes to Lille, Mulhouse, Lyon, and Strasbourg from New York.

- Sabena Airlines, in cooperation with American Express offered first class and business class passengers traveling from New York, Boston, Chicago, or Atlanta to Brussels, Belgium, a free seat for a friend traveling on the same itinerary. The ticket had to be paid for with an American Express card. No advance purchase was required.

- Lufthansa gave a 50 percent discount on companion trips for round-trip bookings for first class and business class travelers. The offer was valid for anyone traveling from Florida or the Caribbean to any Lufthansa destination in West or East Germany, including Berlin.

- Pan Am, in a joint venture with American Express, offered discounts and free companion tickets to transcontinental passengers. Tickets needed to be purchased on an American Express card. Travelers taking a round-trip transcontinental Pan Am flight from major United States east and west coast cities received 50 percent off the cost of a coach companion ticket to any Pan Am city in Europe. By taking two qualifying transcontinental flights, travelers earned a free clipper class companion ticket to Europe.

- Members of United's Mileage Plus frequent flyer program offered members who completed three trips between the United States and Frankfurt or Paris, a two-for-one certificate. The certificate entitled two passengers to travel on one Mileage Plus free saver fare on United Airlines.

- American Savings Bank and Continental teamed up on an offer whereby putting $20,000 into a qualifying American Savings certificate of deposit (CD) entitled you to a free companion ticket when a Continental ticket was purchased to the same destination. Buy a $10,000 CD, and save 75 percent off the companion ticket fare. A $2,500 CD entitled flyers to a 50 percent discount off the companion ticket.

- Coast Federal Bank gave certificates good for two tickets on Northwest Airlines to customers opening a $5,000 CD, a $2,500 savings account, or a $1,000 checking account. The certificates entitled travelers to fly to over 200 Northwest destinations in the Continental United States and Alaska for $124 per person each way.

- Burger King Kid's Club and TWA joined up for a promotion allowing children age 2 to 11 to fly with an adult passenger for just $99 more. A special $99 companion certificate was awarded for enrolling in the Burger King Kid's Club.

Companion fares are usually offered for a limited time only, with published blackout periods during peak-season travel times.

SPECIAL MEMBER DISCOUNTS

The nation's airlines also grant members of certain groups discounts on air travel. These include senior citizens (see separate section on senior citizen fares), the clergy, Red Cross workers, retired military personnel, medical students, and children. In most cases the amount of the discount depends on the specific route being taken, rather than a set percentage off the published fare.

For example, Alaska Airlines gives discounts for military personnel and government employees. American Airlines gives a 50 percent military personnel discount, government employee discounts, and a few student discounts on international fares. Pan Am has a student fare (full-time students only) on some flights, gives military and government employee discounts, as well as discounts to clergy, job corps trainees, and seamen. United, along with all the other airlines we checked, gives military and government employee discounts and occasional student discounts on European flights. Continental has student discounts in certain markets (mostly East Coast), and gives Red Cross worker discounts in emergency cases. TWA, along with military and government discounts, offers a Getaway Student Discount Card, ($15 for one year; $25 for two years) which gives a 10 percent discount off any published fare to full-time students between the ages of 16 and 26.

FLY THE LESS FAMILIAR/ POPULAR AIRLINE

Airlines with less familiar names—Singapore, Korean, Thai, Royal Jordanian, Cathay Pacific, ANA-All Nippon—tend to offer lower fares than do the more advertised, well known carriers. This also goes for newer airlines that are trying to attract customers for routes previously dominated by the familiar, larger carriers.

Also, some airlines are simply less popular because they've earned the reputation of frequently being late or their service and/or food is not as good as other airlines'. Even flying a particular model aircraft (i.e., the DC–10) may be reason enough for some passengers to avoid an airline. An airline with public relations problems may lower its fares to lure customers back and hopefully prove the media wrong.

HIDDEN CITY STRATEGY

The *hidden city* method takes advantage of the airlines' habit of charging more to fly out of their hub cities than through them. If your destination is a city whose inbound and outbound flights are dominated by a single airline that charges more because of its monopoly, you can book yourself to (or from) a less expensive, less popular destination that connects *through* the more expensive city (the hidden city) and simply get off at that stop and not take the rest of the flight. This undermines the airlines' strategy of improving profitability by charging low rates for travel to low traffic destinations while charging higher rates to the hubs where the demand is higher. (A recent report showed fares were nearly 30 percent higher to hub cities than to airports not dominated by major airlines.)

For example, a recent unrestricted one-way fare from Dallas/Ft. Worth to Phoenix was $393. The same flight, booked from Houston, with a connection in Dallas/Ft. Worth to Phoenix was $207. You could discard the Houston-Dallas/Ft. Worth portion of the ticket, board during the Dallas stop, get off in Phoenix, and save $186. When returning, you would depart in Dallas and never fly the last leg of the original ticket back to Houston.

A *hidden city* fare can be used when booking a flight from Los Angeles to Dallas/Ft.Worth. For example, the regular coach fare is $410. But, by booking the flight from L.A. to San Antonio *via* Dallas/Ft. Worth your fare is lowered to $139. That's a savings of $271.

In addition (even though recent new rules prohibit "throwaway city" flights), because of stiff competition on international routes, many fares to or through foreign cities are actually less expensive than domestic flights. That's because domestic fares have been rising while international fares, on some routes, have dropped. For example, a cheap flight from Dallas to New York could be orchestrated by booking a flight to Toronto with a connection in New York. Fly from Dallas to New York, get off the flight and forget the portion to Toronto. This saves $260 off the unrestricted coach fare of $482 for a direct Dallas-New York flight. Round trip flights to foreign destinations with extra stops ticketed in cities not actually visited can save long distance travelers $1,000 or more.

Hidden city fares drive airlines crazy. They claim this practice violates their rules, and some agents won't book clients on a hidden cities itinerary. Sometimes an airline will cancel return reservations when a customer misses an outbound connection (which they can sometimes catch through their computer systems), so always reconfirm your return reservation. Also, always travel with "carry-on" luggage only, since most airlines refuse to check luggage to any *hidden city.*

On January 1, 1990, the Department of Transportation adopted a new rule prohibiting fictitious stops on itineraries that include *international* flights. This has caused many international business class fares to increase by as much as 25 percent. An example of this is the fare from New York-Tokyo-London-New York that cost $3,379 (business class) in 1989, but following the new rule in 1990, cost $5,056. Since the hidden city ticketing method has enjoyed popular and widespread practice among business travelers, this rule has affected them the most. This comes at an especially difficult time when fares are rising steadily both domestically and abroad because of rising labor and fuel costs.

The publication *Best Fares*, 1111 West Cerbarras Lane, Suite C, Arlington, Texas 76013, provides lists of current hidden city fares as a regular feature.

NESTED TRAVEL:
TWO TRIPS CAN BE CHEAPER THAN ONE

Nested travel (also sometimes called *split-ticketing*) is particularly useful when you want to fly as cheaply as possible, but don't want to stay over a Saturday night as required by most excursion fares. To avoid this trap you can buy two discount tickets, one a round-trip ticket from your city to the destination, the other a round trip ticket from the destination to your city.

For example, an unrestricted round-trip ticket to Chicago from Los Angeles on United costs $1,114. However, a round-trip ticket staying over a Saturday night costs only $343. You can purchase two round-trip tickets for $686, one from L.A. to Chicago and one from Chicago to L.A. You then use the outbound portion of each ticket for your first trip.

If you need to take only one trip to Chicago you save $428. However, if you travel often to Chicago and can plan two trips in advance using both tickets (and appearing to stay over on a Saturday night each time), you save $1,542!! This translates into incredible savings, virtually allowing you to travel for less than free! Unless you are certain of the dates for your "second trip," you should make your "return" reservations several months ahead, although as we mentioned before, we have been able to get on an earlier flight by going "standby," even though our ticket was restricted or "nonchangeable.")

What if you don't need your "second trip" and therefore can't use two roundtrip tickets? While it is true that you still have saved almost 40 percent, there are other alternatives. If you're sick (usually a doctor's note is required), you can either obtain a partial refund or at least an extension of your travel time. Also, some people choose to give away their extra tickets to friends, associates, or relatives or sell them through the classified advertising in local newspapers. Although this is technically against the restrictions on transferring your ticket, many airlines allow this practice to go unchallenged.

As you can imagine, this "double round-trip" method is a great way for frequent business travelers to save money while avoiding the Saturday night stayover.

IF YOU WANT TO GO ONE-WAY

Most of the time if you want to travel one way, you will be required to purchase a full fare ticket. That single one way ticket will probably cost more than a round trip excursion ticket. Check on the round trip promotional fares available, and if they're less than the one way ticket (buy it or use the alternatives we described above to "use" the unneeded ticket).

If you want to travel one way from a destination other than where you are (i.e., you want to take a train from Los Angeles to Chicago, but you want to fly back from Chicago to Los Angeles), be sure to make the Chicago-Los Angeles portion of your ticket the first portion of the ticket with the Los Angeles-Chicago as the return portion. That way the airlines computers won't cancel the first portion of a Los Angeles-Chicago round trip originating in Los Angeles that was never used.

SAVING ON GROUP/VOLUME TRAVEL

Groups can range from families to large corporate groups. Either your personal travel agent, your company travel agent, or sometimes you as an individual can arrange these group fares. We'll start with the smallest group, the family, and grow from there.

Fares for the Family

First of all, a child under the age of two travels for free. This usually applies to only one child per adult. If you have a second child under two, that child usually must pay a child's fare, which is about 80 percent of the economy coach adult fare. However, the child does not have to be traveling with a family member. So if there is another adult in your party or you can find a willing passenger (over 12 years old) who will officially "accompany" the child, you can save the extra fare and claim the child once you've boarded. The only problem is that there is no seat reserved for the child, who must sit on the lap of the adult, if all seats are booked.

The once-common "family fare" is becoming more scarce. However, it can still be found occasionally. Last year, American Airlines and Security Pacific Bank offered a promotion whereby opening an individual retirement account (IRA), an adult could purchase a round- trip economy ticket with a second adult ticket at a 70 percent discount and a maximum of two children tickets at a 90 percent discount each.

This is the usual format for family fares: one adult pays full-fare Business or Economy; spouse and children travel on the same itinerary for substantially reduced rates. It ends up cheaper than if all family members travel Coach excursions, especially for a family of four or more. Also, family plan fares usually have fewer restrictions than Coach excursion fares.

Family fares differ from airline to airline. As recent examples, on some Alaska Airlines routes, one adult paid full Coach fare and family members paid 50 percent of that rate. On some Delta routes, an adult paid full Coach fare while other members of the family paid from $49 to $99 dollars each way. Midway gives a spouse reduction of 10 percent on any fare (see companion fares) in addition to its standard reduction for children. For trips to Florida, (now defunct) Eastern Airlines offered children's fares as low as $29 to $78 round trip for flights to Florida from many U.S. cities. To keep up with the competition, other airlines flying to Florida followed that example, including Pan Am, TWA and Continental. Air Canada recently allowed a spouse or children age 2 to 18 to travel at 50 percent off the regular fare, with the purchase of a full fare business or economy class ticket. Offer was good from most United States destinations to Canada

An example of an international family fare is the "Nipper Tripper" fare offered by Qantas. Buy one adult economy excursion ticket from Los Angeles or San Francisco to Brisbane, Cairns, Melbourne, Sydney, or Townsville ($1,295 at the time of offer), and one child (age 2-12) could travel on the same itinerary for just $295. A second adult traveling paid $895 and could take a child along for the same $295 fare as the first child. This was a limited time offer with restrictions, but it was a very good deal for families traveling with children. It also allowed up to two stops in addition to the final destination.

"Kids fly free" promotions have also been popular in recent years. These are usually offered for a limited time during the summer and carry several restrictions, although the savings warrant the careful planning (with the restrictions adhered to the letter). It's difficult to predict when airlines are going to offer these promotions, but when one announces such a program, you can be sure that the other major airlines will follow suit so as not to miss out on their share of summer travelers.

Fares for Attendees Going to a Meeting, Convention, or Your High School Reunion?

Professional, fraternal, and other organizations can often arrange reduced fares for members attending out-of-town meetings. These fares offer either or both of two options:

1. Thirty to fifty percent reductions from full coach, with no restrictions other than perhaps a short minimum advance-purchase period (to insure blocking out enough seats).

2. Five percent reductions from any published adult fare, including the cheapest excursion, with the Saturday night stay sometimes waived.

Most airlines have a group-travel desk for conventions and meetings. They will usually bend over backwards to accommodate you, suggest economical routing, and may even make competing air and ground reservations.

Sometimes the organizer of a convention or seminar will name an "official" airline and list it in the reservation packet. If you qualify for the packet, you qualify for the fare. Meeting fares are generally valid from several days before the actual meeting begins to several days after it ends. They also usually qualify for frequent-flyer mileage credit but not for upgrades.

Some travel agencies will compile information on all major meetings in cities their clients visit frequently. They then offer their clients (who may or may not qualify as attendees) the reduced meeting fare. Although this technically is a misuse of the intended purpose of the fare, there is almost no way an airline can check if an individual traveler on a meeting fare is actually attending the specified meeting. Travel agents can get the specific "booking code" that identifies the ticket from an advance program or meeting brochure. (Gale Research publishes two directories, *Trade Shows Worldwide* and *Seminars Directory,* which are current guides to thousands of trade shows, exhibitions, association conventions, workshops, and seminars. The books are available by calling: (800) 877-GALE or look for them at the public library.)

Fares for Large Companies and Corporations

Costs for business travel have been rising steadily for several years. This includes costs for lodgings car rental, air fares, and meals, which virtually doubled during the 1980s. Air fares alone have exploded since the 1986 airline industry consolidation. Unrestricted tickets, which most business travelers book, rose 96 percent in the last decade. In 1989 alone, airfares rose 16 percent.

The only relief that has been offered to business travelers recently has been by a few airlines that have been forced by poor sales and the industry's slump as a whole to ease fare restrictions and let business flyers in on the "deals." For example, some travelers no longer must stay over a Saturday to get cheap fares out of major markets such as Atlanta, New York, and Miami. Instead of Saturday, some airlines require that the traveler stay over a Friday night instead. Originally started by smaller airlines competing with the majors, some business traveler concessions are now being made by the larger airlines that have been forced to join in the popular move towards cheap business traveler tickets.

Last year, several major airlines announced a new strategy for business travelers. The airlines offered new "corporate rate" prices for first class travel that were 15 to 35 percent below the full fare coach rates. Whereas the industry average full coach rate from Atlanta to Chicago was $379 and the average first class fare $565, the new "corporate rate" for the same route was $313, and if purchased three days in advance only $247.

A growing number of companies are saving big money on employee travel costs by negotiating special deals with the airlines for volume travel. Corporate discounting isn't new, but recently, more liberal deals with airlines and hotels are becoming the norm. The use of so-called "negotiated air fares" jumped to nearly 15 percent of all airplane tickets in 1989 versus just under 1 percent in early 1988. It is estimated that big companies are getting special rates on more than one third of their airline tickets.

Negotiated airfares can be 5 to 40 percent lower than discounted fares available to regular travelers. Since airline deregulation, there has been a surge in corporate discounting due to the fierce competition among airlines. Whereas corporate discounting used to be a subject not openly talked about by airlines, most will admit to the practice nowadays.

In the past, airlines didn't want to publicize these deals for fear that leisure and small business travelers would resent the bigger business travelers paying much less. Also, now that these cuts have become such a widespread practice, the airlines (and hotels) need to make up the money on the cuts from somewhere, and that somewhere might be from the pockets of the "regular" travelers.

Nonetheless, even small companies are getting special fares as the competition for the larger corporations gets hotter.

For example, Midway Airlines will fly an employee of one large computer corporation between Philadelphia and Minneapolis (one way) for $200, which is sharply lower than the regular coach fare of $327. That discount alone saves the corporation $360,000 annually.

CHARTER FLIGHTS AND CHARTER AIRLINES

Several years ago, the only way to fly economically (especially for a family or group) was to use charter flights. But due to deregulation with more and more competitive pricing and choice of pricing levels by major airlines, the once strong charter market was severely cut into by the competition of the majors. Many charter operators became consolidators (see the section on consolidators in Chapter 5), offering discount tickets on the major airlines. However, charters today can still offer a good alternative for some trips.

Charter versus Commercial Airlines

Basically, the difference between charters and discount flights on commercial airlines are as follows:

I. When you fly with a major airline, your contract is between you and the airline. Legally, if anything goes wrong, your recourse is with the airline. On a charter flight you are contracting with a wholesale tour operator who, in turn, has subcontracted with an airline to do the actual flying. If anything goes wrong with your charter flight, you have only the tour operator, not, the airline to turn to. If you have any doubts about the financial stability or track record of the tour operator, check first with the U.S. Department of Transportation, Office of Consumer Affairs, (202) 366–2220, to see if any complaints have been filed against the operator.

2. Most charter flights only fly their routes once or twice a week, offering less flexibility and choice than a major airline with daily departures. The limited choice of return dates may mean less or more time at a destination than you'd planned. However, sometimes the charter flight is the only nonstop flight available, not requiring plane changes or extra stops (especially for international travel where an airline's planes always stop at a U.S. hub or European gateway). This alone could save you several hours and considerable hassle in traveling (especially with a family or larger group).

   However, if you like to scout around a plane for an empty seat or two with the chance of stretching out on a longer flight, don't count on it with a charter. Because of the way the seats are sold, charter flights are almost always full or close to capacity. Airlines flying charter trips normally have only one or two check-in personnel at the charter flight desk, so plan to spend some extra time in line checking in, and don't expect to see those roaming, friendly airline "hosts" and "hostesses" eager to assist you in answering your questions.

3. Economically, charter airlines have a lower average cost per seat than major airlines. Therefore, they can charge lower average fares. Usually all the seats on a charter flight are priced exactly the same, down to the last available seat. This is a significant difference from major airlines, which have several pricing levels, the lowest of which might be lower than the charter price, but also may be available on only a very limited seating basis and likely to be sold out very quickly, leaving you the choice of the higher priced tickets.

Other Differences in Charter Flights

Many charter programs focus on Europe, especially during the summer months. In fact, it's often very difficult to distinguish between the charter price for tickets and a consolidator's discount price with a major airline. Often both kinds of tickets are sold by the same people and promoted in ads that don't specify which is which.

Unfortunately, consolidator discounts aren't available on most domestic flights. On these flights (i.e., Hawaii, the Caribbean, Rocky Mountain ski areas), the charters are mainly competing with the lowest priced excursion fares on major airlines. During a peak season, a charter flight may be the only way to reach these areas for a decently discounted price.

For example, during ski season the lowest round-trip excursion fare from Los Angeles to Salt Lake City (requiring seven-day advance purchase, Saturday night stay, traveling on Monday afternoon through Thursday morning only) was $231. The next best fare was $450 for a nonrefundable ticket, requiring a Saturday night stay and a 50 percent penalty for cancellation. The nonrestricted coach fare was $752. However, a charter company flying round-trip nonstop jet service from Los Angeles to Salt Lake City cost only $178. Which one would you take?

There is also a stigma of uncertainty surrounding charter flights:

- Uncertainty over whether the flight will actually take off if there aren't enough seats sold and the operator decides to cancel the flight and replace it with discount tickets on a major airline.

- Uncertainty as to whether the price of tickets, when first announced, will possibly be revised closer to the flight time if too many seats remain empty. Charter operators can raise the price of a fare by as much as 10 percent up to 10 days before departure. Or they can lower the fare at the last minute in a final attempt to fill empty seats.

- Uncertainty as to the reliability of the charter tour operator and whether your prepaid dollars are actually being used for airfare.

- Uncertainty as to an unanticipated itinerary change, i.e. a tour operator who compensates for low bookings by combining two or more charters that were originally promoted as separate programs, sometimes resulting in marathon flight times between desired destinations.

We strongly advise that charter flights be booked through major tour operators who have operated their schedules for several years without an unusually high rate of cancellation or major modification in advertised routes. Trip-interruption travel insurance is also recommended to cover the risk of operator failure as well as other contingencies that might cause you to lose some or all of your payment.

When paying for a charter flight or tour, the check should be made out to the escrow bank account of the tour operator (usually found in very small print in the operator's brochure). Write "For Deposit Only" on the back of the check and the destination, dates, and other details on the front. This forces the operator to deposit the check in that account and you are better protected against cancellation of the trip or failure of the tour operator. This should be done in the case of buying consolidator tickets as well.

Another difference between charter planes and those flown by major airlines is that charters are special aircraft configured for charter service. What that translates into is more seats, resulting in cramped, crowded seating often somewhat worse than the coach/economy section of a major airline. A long international flight may turn into the "Flight from Hell" if you end up in the middle seat next to an overweight, talkative passenger or an especially rambunctious child. Recently, several of the major European charter airlines have begun offering optional premium class seating on some routes for a moderate price increase. These include Balair (Switzerland), Condor (Germany), LTU (Germany), and Martinair (Dutch). Even though these fares are around 20 to 35 percent higher than economy charter rates, they are still a fraction of the business or first class fares on a major airline.

Below are a couple of specialized circumstances where we recommend using charter flights:

1. Wait for the last minute and book a seat or seats from a company (or through a club) that has been unable to fill its plane. Some charters, in order to fill these seats, will drop their prices for those willing to wait until the last minute to make their travel plans. There are, in fact, several "last-minute travel clubs" (see the section on Last-Minute Travel later in this chapter), which work with the charters to fill those unsold seats at discounted prices cheaper than the advertised charter price. In reality, many of these "last-minute" flights are available several weeks ahead of the departure date. Often it is a packaged tour that is available, rather than a flight alone. Even then, the total cost with the extra discount can be less than a normal air fare alone.

2. Choose a charter that offers a nonstop route where no major airline provides one. (For example, Miami-Zurich or New York-Cardiff). The shorter travel time and reduced hassle on a nonstop can offset the minor disadvantages encountered with most charter companies, especially if the tour operator is an established, reputable one with a reliable record.

Below are major tour operators marketing charter flights in the United States and their phone numbers:

Charter Company	Telephone Number
Amber Tours	(800) 262-3701
American Trans Air	(313) 591-1020
Char-Tours	(800) 323-4444

continued. . .

Club America Vacations (sells only to travel agents, will not accept calls from public).	
Club de Vacaciones (Spain only)	(800) 648-0404
Council Charter	(800) 223-7402
DER (sells only to travel agents)	(800) 782-2424
Fantasy Holidays	(800) 645-2555
Ferien-Service Swiss Travel	(305) 591-1566
continued. . .	
GO Voyages	(212) 481-7500
GWV Intl. Weekends	(800) 225-5498
Homeric	(800) 223-5570
Martinair	(800) 366-4655
Morris Air Service	(800) 444-5660
Pleasure Break/Charter Travel (sells only to travel agents)	(800) 777-1566
Sceptre Charters (Europe only)	(800) 221-0924
Schwaben Intl.	(212) 432-0116
Sunbird Vacations (sells only to travel agents)	(408) 452-0202
Travac	(800) 872-8800
Travel Charter (Europe, Mexico)	(800) 521-5267

BARTER TRAVEL

Travel and entertainment businesses frequently find it to their advantage to issue credit to their suppliers or employees for future services in lieu of total or partial cash payment. This, in turn, allows the suppliers or employees to travel free on the airline or get certain services (at hotels or restaurants) free or at deeply discounted rates.

Barter is so common in the travel industry that many suppliers accumulate far more travel credit than they can use. What these companies do is try to convert the excess travel credits into something more useful to them, either by selling it for cash or trading it again for something else they need. Generally speaking, use of bartered credit is a legal form of trade and does not violate any airline rules.

Individuals can buy bartered credit through travel clubs, barter exchanges or a coupon broker. You can look them up in your local newspaper or yellow pages under "Barter" or "Trade Exchanges." We have also listed below some of the travel clubs and other sources of bartered air travel credit. This is a very fluid market with the availability of discounts always changing and being replaced with new barter credits.

Most bartered travel credit is in the form of a credit balance for the total dollar value of goods or services involved in a trade. As the credit is used, the value is deducted from the balance. Another form of barter credit is scrip, which can be used for payment in lieu of currency. Scrip is more convenient than keeping track of a credit balance, but its major drawback is that you can't get "change" in scrip, i.e., if your charge is less than the lowest available scrip denomination, you get back neither cash or scrip.

Some bartered credit is unrestricted and can be used just like cash. In the case of most airline credit, the amount can be applied to any published fare, limited only by those restrictions applying to the fare selected. However, there are other limitations to bartered travel credits. Tickets/vouchers can be issued only through the travel club or barter exchange, not through a travel agency. Also, bartered airline tickets are good only on the issuing airline. They are not exchangeable for use on another carrier if your flight is delayed or canceled.

The easiest and simplest way for individuals to obtain bartered travel credit is to buy it at a discounted price. Discounts can range up to 50 percent. There are several travel clubs that specialize in obtaining bartered travel credit and merchandising it to travelers.

There are also barter exchanges around the country that can give information and handle credit for airline tickets, cruise space, tours, hotel accommodations, and restaurant meals. These organizations will match your offer and what you want to exchange them for with those of others, taking a small percent of the transaction as a fee. Virtually any product or service can become a potential source of barter, from baby sitting services to medical services to computer products or household items. Occasionally, barter exchanges will sell travel credit for cash at discount prices, but much of the credit is sold at or near list prices. When an exchange offers discounts for a cash sale, they are usually in the 10 to 20 percent range. That may still be a good value for domestic airline tickets since other discounts are uncommon. However, for international tickets you may be better off going through a consolidator or discount agency.

Other than a few club programs, barter is about the only way to obtain discounts of 20 to 25 percent on domestic airlines, although the choice of airlines is limited. Depending on what you have to offer, you may be able to obtain your air tickets and other travel values at very low out-of-pocket costs.

The table on the following page is a list of barter exchanges, associations and travel clubs that specialize in bartered air travel credit.

TRAVEL COUPONS, EXCHANGES, AND TICKET BROKERS

Ticket brokers buy and sell frequent-flyer awards, called *coupons*. When a buyer wants to purchase an award, the broker calls the seller and asks the seller to submit the paperwork required by the airline to issue the award in the buyer's name. The buyer pays the broker a "retail" price that is usually well under the airline's published price. The broker pays the seller a lower

Barter Source	Telephone Number
Barter Network	(203) 874-8962
Barter News (Newsletter)	(714) 495-6529
Bartermax	(617) 769-3400
Discount Club of America	(800) 321-9587
IGT (In Good Taste)	(800) 444-8872
Int'l Reciprocal Trade Association	(703) 759-1473
LPC Media (deals only in trading between companies)	(619) 756-3003
The Travel Broker (coupon broker that also sells bartered travel credit)	(214) 985-8528
Travel World Leisure Club	(212) 244-3562

"wholesale" price. The seller makes a profit, the broker makes a profit, and the buyer gets a good deal on his air travel.

Savings on frequent-flyer awards are not that great for economy class tickets for domestic travel; however, for use as upgrades to business class and first-class travel, the savings can be substantial. These awards, in fact, remain the only way most travelers can afford the extra comfort and service of business or first class. And for travelers who may occasionally want an inexpensive coach ticket (up to 30 percent below list) without an advance purchase or Saturday-night-stay requirement, keeping an "open" coupon on hand makes good sense.

Most airlines allow members of their frequent-flyer programs to transfer coupons to family members, friends, or even business associates. The problem comes when the award is sold, which violates the rules of virtually all airlines. Each coupon specifically states that it cannot be traded for cash, and airlines can confiscate a ticket if they believe a coupon changed hands for money somewhere along the way.

However, the American Association of Discount Travel Brokers claims that this occurs less than 1 percent of the time. As insurance some ticket brokers will give a refund if the ticket is not honored. If your ticket is confiscated, then you will need to buy a new full fare ticket. Some people who have been caught and forced to buy replacement tickets use a credit card for payment, then refuse to pay the bill on the grounds that the coupon ticket should have been honored. This technique may put them in a slightly better bargaining position with the airline, which then has to decide whether it is worth it to contest the issue in court.

The exchange/broker system began in 1981, when the first award program was announced and some smart entrepreneurs realized that many flyers would eventually amass many more bonus miles than they could possibly use and thus would be happy to sell the awards, presenting both of them with a new money-making opportunity. This has turned out to be especially true for business flyers who chose to sell their flight credit rather than use it on tickets for themselves, family, or friends. Today there are about 50 brokers who trade an estimated $25 million in tickets a year.

The following list includes brokers who deal in frequent-flyer awards and bump tickets. Some also sell consolidator tickets.

Exchange/Broker	Telephone Number
Airline Coupon Co.	(800) 354-4489
American Coupon Exchange	(714) 644-4112
Coupon Bank	(800) 292-9250
Creative Travel	(215) 354-9669
Delta Assistance	(800) 443-3599
continued. . .	

Fly in Class	(800) 448-8000
Flyers Choice	(213) 395-2436
Go in Class	(312) 236-9696
Int'l Air Coupon Exchange	(800) 558-0053
Platinum World Travel	(800) 877-2835
Texas Traveler	(800) 877-2855
The Travel Broker	(214) 985-8528
Travel Creations	(800) 843-0737
Travel Mart-Los Angeles	(213) 471-5222
Travel Solutions	(907) 274-2359
World Plus	(907) 451-1900

Coupons sold through brokers are mainly from five major airlines: American, Continental, Delta, Northwest, and United. These coupons provide for travel on the issuing airline and, in some cases, foreign airline partners.

Travelers who buy coupons should follow a few simple rules and warnings:

- Always use a credit card to purchase your ticket, giving you some protection should anything go wrong. A few brokers, realizing the consumers recourse in this case, do not take credit cards. If they don't, choose a different broker who does.

- If possible find out the vital statistics (name, address, etc.) of the original coupon holder and memorize them. You might even make up a believable relationship between yourself and the seller.

- Buy "bump tickets" for domestic flights. These are tickets that have been issued as consolation prizes to passengers bumped from overcrowded flights. These tickets typically allow either a certain dollar value of travel or travel anywhere within the contiguous 48 states served by the airline. They are generally transferable with no rules against cash sales. Most cost between $350 and $500. However, some bump tickets are good for standby travel only with reservations allowed no more than 24 or 48 hours in advance.

- Buy tickets only from experienced brokers. At the least they will have the knowledge to properly transfer coupons. Avoid individual sellers such as those advertising in the classified sections of the local newspapers.

- Always check published SuperSaver and excursion fares (restricted, advanced purchase fares) before deciding a coupon is the best deal. Special promotional fares, international fares, and wholesalers' prices (through airline consolidators) are sometimes equal to or better than coupon prices. Also coupons do not have the immediate flexibility of full-fare tickets. Coupon holders cannot switch airlines if flights are canceled or delayed. Few carriers allow extra stopovers and coupons for one-way flights are usually not available.

- Keep in mind, too, that the greatest savings are when coupons are used for business class and first class travel. Also, how much you save depends on the length of the trip you take using a coupon. Coupons are issued for travel within or between zones, without regard to trip mileage. A coupon good for a first class trip within the contiguous United States could be used for a round-trip ticket between Los Angeles and Orlando or Los Angeles and San Diego; a coupon for European travel can be used for Los Angeles-Tel Aviv or New York-Amsterdam. A recent first class fare on a round-trip Los Angeles-Tel Aviv ticket was $6,824.

Compare this to $4,110 for a round-trip ticket from New York to Amsterdam, and you see that you get a lot more "mileage" from your coupon going the longer route.

There have been several developments in frequent-flyer programs over the past couple of years that have lead to predictions of an end to the coupon market. However, despite changes in program rules, lawsuits, and intensified airline enforcement, coupon brokers are still proliferating and profiting from a continuing demand for coupons. Even though there are more "blackout dates" and "blackout periods," higher mileage requirements for certain first class trips, and fewer seats allocated to coupon users, using coupons continues to be a popular, available, money-saving option for the traveling public.

FLY FOR LESS: BUY FOOD AND PRODUCTS, USE YOUR CREDIT CARD, OR ORDER FROM A CATALOG

In order to offer more benefits, perks, and services, several consumer outlets have created reciprocal agreements with the airlines, offering varying forms of coupons, discounts, certificates, and mileage awards to the users and buyers of their services and products.

Since 1986, when TWA offered valuable discount coupons through mail-order catalogs, several airlines and catalog companies have become partners in such offerings. One recent one was with Pan Am and several mail order catalogs. For $25 (plus one other purchase from the catalog) a buyer received a coupon good for either a discount or an upgrade. The coupon allowed the user a 25 percent discount on a domestic ticket costing $175 or more each way, or a ticket to Western Europe or South America costing $200 or more each way. Coupons were also used to upgrade domestic coach tickets costing $175 or more each way, or an economy ticket to Western Europe or Caracas costing $400 or more each way.

Travelers who bought unrestricted coach tickets saved hundreds of dollars using a coupon for a discount. Coupons were also a good deal for upgrading long distance domestic trips and for European travel.

Catalogs participating in the above promotion included: Competitive Edge, Diamond Essence, Great Living, Gump's, Horchow, Trifles, Norm Thompson, Orvis, The Sharper Image, Trend-Lines, and The Wine Enthusiast.

TWA also ran a similar promotion with certificates good for upgrades from any coach/economy, or excursion ticket to business or first class or 25 percent discounts on any TWA flights. The certificates needed to be purchased by a certain date with travel completed within four months of the final purchase date. Four mail-order catalogs, Grand Finale, Horchow, S.G.F., and Trifles, teamed up with TWA for this cooperative marketing effort. Continental offered a similar certificate program with upgrade options on domestic flights and discounts valid on any Continental routes. Certificates could be purchased through several mail order catalogs including Brookstone, Horchow Collection, Leichtung and Norm Thompson.

Another successful partnership has been between supermarkets and airlines. Examples of some recent airline/supermarket promotions are:

- Lucky stores in California offered a tie-in between themselves, Ask Mr. Foster travel agencies, and USAir. This promotion was aimed at northern California residents who could exchange $100 worth of supermarket receipts for travel certificates good for coach round-trip USAir or Piedmont flights. With the certificate, a ticket anywhere in the United States cost just $259, or in the western United States, $159. The certificates could be used to buy tickets for someone other than the person who obtained it.

- Lucky Stores found the northern California promotion so popular that a similar program was offered in southern California with Delta Airlines (Save at Lucky, Save on Delta) where receipts for purchases could be exchanged for certificates good for travel valid for approximately six months.

- Von's Grocery Stores in California offered a "25-percent-off discount coupon" from USAir to customers who purchased $100 in groceries.

- TWA and two Midwest grocery store chains, Harvest Foods (located in Arkansas and Wichita, Kansas), and Homeland Foods (located in Oklahoma and north Texas) offered customers similar "25-percent-off" discount certificates for TWA flights.

- Midway Airlines and Alpha Beta food stores in the Los Angeles area joined the airline bandwagon by offering two Midway travel certificates in exchange for $50 in register receipts. The certificates entitled passengers to fly from Los Angeles to Chicago (plus 18 other Midwest cities) for $99 each way, and to other Midway destinations for $129 and $149 each way. Passengers outside of California could also take advantage of the offer because travel on the certificates was valid to or from the Midwest destinations included in the promotion. Midway also entered into a similar promotion with ACME Grocery Stores based in Philadelphia.

In a recent offer, travelers could save up to $120 by purchasing Procter & Gamble products and flying American Airlines. Participants received a $30 certificate good on a round-trip coach ticket of $290 or more for each two participating Procter & Gamble brands they used. A new offer by Kelloggs cereals awarded certificates valid for 25 percent off TWA coach travel including Hawaii, Europe and the Caribbean. Customers who purchased 5 boxes of "Raisin Bran," "Squares," or "Just Right" needed to mail in the U.P.C. codes and a special mail-in voucher to receive their discount certificates by mail.

Retail stores have also gotten into the act selling certificates for discounts and upgrades. The May Company southern California stores sold travel certificates for $25 for upgrades and discounts on certain TWA flights. Called Travel Premium Certificates, they were also offered (good only for discounts, not upgrades) free to anyone enrolling or renewing membership in Travel Channel Concierge, a travel club. Membership in the club, whose main focus is discounts on hotels, resorts, condo rentals, and cruises is $69.95. Either type of Travel Premium Certificate was good for a 25 percent discount on certain domestic and international flights. However, there were blackout periods on travel to Europe and high minimum qualifying fares that made the certificates less valuable than they appeared at first glance.

Nearly every major credit card company offers cardholders bonus points for a specific amount of dollar charged to the credit card. The points can be redeemed for frequent-flyer mileage programs or used for merchandise, travel awards or travel programs of hotels or car rental companies. They also occasionally have special promotions with airlines. Two recent example of credit card/airline promotions are:

- Holders of Discover® Financial Services card were offered Value Finder coupons worth $50 off any published United Airlines round-trip fare of $300 or more, and $35 off any published fare of $175 or more.

- Passengers who purchased MasterCard® Travelers Checks were eligible to send away for certificates worth $40 to $80 (depending on the ticket price level) on American Airlines domestic flights.

Since all airlines (as well as their partners) participating in co-op promotions such as these are looking for the greatest response, they run full page ads in major metropolitan newspapers in the daily news sections and Sunday travel sections, and in national magazines such as *Time, Newsweek,* and *People.* Also check the announcements that come with your credit card statements and frequent flyer news updates

Remember, always compare what you are saving with coupons and certificates to the lowest available excursion fare during the periods of travel when the certificates are valid.

WRAP YOURSELF UP
IN A PACKAGE TOUR

A package tour is a combination of travel services (hotels, land and/or air transportation, meals, gratuities, sightseeing tours, etc.) that have been combined for the convenience of the traveler. They are usually offered at an all-inclusive "package price." Package tours are designed and marketed by wholesale tour operators then sold by travel agents to their customers.

What is the best reason to choose a package tour? Simple—to save money. Savings can add up to several hundred dollars per couple (it's always cheaper to travel with someone or be willing to double up with someone else traveling with the tour). By contracting in bulk for hotels, transportation, sightseeing, and other services a tour operator can achieve substantial savings. Travelers buying everything for themselves individually at the retail rate would end up paying much more.

Also, there are times, especially during peak periods, when tour operators (because they buy in volume) can guarantee reservations and space that is very difficult for individuals to obtain without planning far in advance. Tours save on planning and organizing and are especially helpful to someone who has not experienced international travel and does not speak a foreign language.

Some people still think a package tour means a regimented, highly scheduled, overly planned vacation. This is no longer the case. The fact is that tours encompass a tremendous spectrum of tastes, interests, and travel styles, from the most meticulously preplanned escorted tours to free-wheeling spontaneous fly/drive holidays. The choices in tours are as varied as there are places to go.

There are a few drawbacks to package tours, however. Some do have rushed sightseeing schedules. Sometimes a "full American breakfast" turns out to be coffee and rolls, not exactly what you expected. Remember, what you see is what you get. There are usually few, if any, substitutions or free choices on a package tour.

Also, when dealing with big travel companies patience is often a virtue. It can be difficult to get through to someone with authority to help with a problem you may be experiencing. Make sure that when you do reach a responsible employee you write down their name, keep notes on your conversations, keep copies of any letters that you may need to write. Prior to departure, make sure you have read all the fine print in the tour brochure and understand all the rules, regulations, disclaimers, and know everything that is being included or left out.

Be aware that not all package tours are a bargain. Take time to compare prices when considering a package. Find the cheapest airfare and hotel rates for the same or similar accommodations. Add on a fair value for the other services offered: meals, airport transfers, sightseeing, etc.

A package tour should be a better deal than if you were traveling independently, because the tour operators are buying at wholesale rates. If you are looking for convenience in planning, scheduling, and getting from place to place, and find that the tour price is equal to or slightly less than the retail price, consider the tour and avoid the hassles of a do-it-yourself trip. Independent travel in some cases can be cheaper than a tour, especially during an off-season when there are lots of hotel and fly/drive bargains. But it's a personal choice as to what kind of trip you enjoy most that will make the difference in choosing independent over tour travel.

The United States Tour Operators Association, (212) 944-5727, is a member organization that offers information and tips on tour travel. They publish a guide listing their members, pro-grams, services, and destinations.

Tours are offered by all kinds of groups who enlist the expertise of travel agents or professional tour operators. You can travel with a local professional, cultural or educational group, in which case you're likely to meet others who share your interests.

Several tour operators advertise, "Fly Free" or "Stay Free" vacations and tours. If you purchase certain air/land packages and accommodations, the flight or hotel portion of your trip is free. (For examples of these offers, see More Ways to Fly Free in Chapter 3.) These promotions can save money, but as always, the final cost of the package should be evaluated carefully. If the accommodations and rates are comparable to what you would choose and end up paying if you were traveling independently, then you could be getting a very good deal since the airfare is "thrown in." However, even with the air fare included, paying for deluxe accommodations at two to three times the price you would normally pay could cost you a lot more than if you flew economy yourself and stayed at a less expensive hotel.

LAST-MINUTE TRAVEL

Last-Minute Travel can mean:

- Emergency travel (in the case of a death or illness).

- Standby travel using "bump" tickets.

- Actually standing by (with a ticket in your pocket but hoping for a cheaper way to go).

- Using tickets obtained from travel agencies that specialize in "last-minute travel."

If you have to take an unexpected trip because of a family illness or death, almost all U.S. airlines will waive restrictions on excursions fares when you tell them your reason for traveling. You will need documentation from a doctor, hospital, or mortician (usually acceptable after your return) in order to convince the airline of your emergency. Additionally, some airlines (Continental, Northwest, USAir) offer special "bereavement" fares, which are cheaper than regular fares.

In addition, there are several charities and airline employee groups that will arrange (and pay for) what is known as "compassionate" air transportation. These are for passengers and their families who need and can't afford to travel to special medical facilities available in only a few cities. One group that specializes in compassionate air travel is AirLifeLine, (916) 446-0995.

Bump coupons (see section on coupons and ticket brokers earlier in this chapter) on some airlines permit last-minute travel to most routes the airline flies in the United States. A few carriers permit such coupons to be bought and sold. You can buy them directly from another traveler (the one who was bumped originally) or through a coupon broker. They generally only allow reservations between 24 and 48 hours in advance.

Most standby fares for domestic travel offer little savings compared to regular advertised fares. However, you can standby for flights between North America and Europe and obtain very inexpensive tickets (even during peak travel months.) In addition, there are "standby brokers" who receive last-minute empty seats from an airline and sell them at substantially discounted prices. The key to this kind of air travel is flexibility, since availability for any specific date and destination is a matter of chance, and standby flights are for one-way travel only. Examples of standby brokers are Access, (212) 333-7280, and Airhitch, (212) 864-2000.

If you are flexible, another way to obtain inexpensive tickets is by joining a last-minute travel club. There are several clubs that specialize in last-minute cruise travel, packages, and escorted tours. A few offer air-only charters. Some clubs charge yearly dues (between $30 and $50) and some are free. They notify members of upcoming bargains as they become available through periodic newsletters, post card mailings, or toll-free numbers giving recorded messages on current trips. Despite their name, last-minute travel clubs have knowledge of and access to seats on commercial and tour flights several weeks ahead of departure dates, so you actually don't have to wait until the last minute.

The table below lists some last-minute travel clubs specializing in standby and last minute air travel.

Last-Minute Service	Telephone Number
Encore Short Notice	(800) 638-8976
Last Minute Travel	(617) 267-9800
Moment's Notice	(212) 486-0503
Stand-Buys Limited	(800) 255-1488
Vacations To Go	(800) 624-7338
Worldwide Discount Travel Club	(305) 534-2082

You can also buy last-minute travel from some travel agencies that obtain these bargains by negotiating individual deals with travel wholesalers who have more packages than they can sell. The advantage to buying through a travel agency is the savings on the annual club fee. However, you won't receive regular updates and news bulletins from a retail travel agent who only books last-minute travel as a sideline.

In response to the popularity of last-minute travel, TWA recently started its own last-minute travel club called Breakaway Club. Dues are $100 for singles and $175 for couples or one member traveling alone or with a companion. Members receive notices of discounted flights and tours from their area, with airfares generally lower than the cheapest available coach excursions (but not always as low as the very-short-term specials available periodically on certain routes). For example, transcontinental trips are as low as $240 compared with about $350 for most excursions. Flights offered are not always to the most desirable destinations, and times, dates, and connections are sometimes inconvenient. You end up trading dollars for convenience and choice with Breakaway Club or any last-minute club offering.

Finally, some smaller airlines offer comparatively low unrestricted fares on certain routes, with the major lines often matching them on routes where they compete. Recently, Virgin Atlantic offered a "Late Late Saver" one-way fare of $149 from Miami and New York to London, with seats available starting the day before departure. However, in most cases even the lower unrestricted fares are higher than those requiring advance purchase.

CHAPTER 3
FLYING FOR FREE

FLYING FOR FREE

In the preceding sections, we have shown you ways to save on air travel, including tours and traveling with others. In this chapter we explain some of the amazingly simple and generally unknown avenues of flying absolutely free. In fact, most free travel requires no special skills, credentials, or contacts. If traveling for free is your goal, we'll show you the ways to reach it. For example, traveling as a travel writer, a tour leader, group organizer or as an air courier are just a few.

TRAVEL FREE AS A TRAVEL WRITER

If you have a flair for writing, you have a good chance of paying for your travels by selling your experience, unusual story, photos, etc., to publications and newspapers that are looking for a new point of view about a different place. Travel is one of the biggest industries in today's world. People are hungry to know about new and interesting places and learn about the experiences of others in those places. Remember, *your* point of view is a *new* point of view, even if the places you've visited have been written about many times before. In addition to the many consumer-oriented magazines and newsletters that specialize in travel, there are hundreds of clubs, community groups, and organizations that will pay to hear lectures and see slides and photos about someone's adventures.

There are also many publications that are not specifically aimed toward travelers, but that accept travel articles and columns because it is a subject of interest to most readers. These include "women's" magazines, sports-oriented magazines, general-interest magazines and national newspapers, mature adult magazines, club and organization newsletters, and magazines focusing on specific metropolitan areas, such as *Los Angeles* magazine, *Dallas*, *California*, *Arizona Living*, etc. Daily and weekly newspapers also welcome features about new and interesting places to travel and points of interest.

Becoming a travel writer with the goal of traveling for free can be either a full- or part-time career. Obviously, it is something that takes some practice (writing, speaking, or taking photos) and requires a commitment to learning the markets in which you want to sell your travel stories. But it is a great opportunity to pay for your travels by sharing your personal experiences.

To learn more about becoming a travel writer, check for adult education classes at your local community college, high school, or adult learning center. Often they offer courses in becoming a travel writer taught by experts who have done it for many years. For those who have made a career of travel writing and have earned positions as regular contributors, columnists, or circuit lecturers, free traveling has become a way of life.

TRAVEL FREE BY ORGANIZING YOUR OWN GROUP

Another way to travel free is by organizing your own tour or group. If you can enlist enough people, you can get your entire trip—long or short—for free. Some travel agencies recruit teachers who receive a free trip if they bring six students. With 12 students, the teacher's spouse also travels free. Traveling free as a teacher is a very popular way to see and go places that would otherwise be financially prohibitive.

TRAVEL FREE BY ORGANIZING A SPECIAL-INTEREST GROUP

Similarly, anyone willing to organize folks for a special-interest tour can earn a free trip from the travel agent who helps puts the tour together and books it. For example:

- A wine aficionado might organize a group to the French wine country.

- A church member might enlist others to take a religious pilgrimage to a Holy Land.

- An opera buff might arrange a trip to Vienna.

- A tennis enthusiast might get friends to meet at Wimbledon.

Special-interest trips focus on photography, architecture, theater, music, history, golf, food, or anything that people have a special passion for. Working with a creative travel agent or directly with airline group travel representatives, hotels, and resorts can produce some fantastic trips that are 100 percent free to you.

TRAVEL FREE AS A TOUR ESCORT OR GUIDE

There are many tour operators both in the United States and abroad, who are always looking for interesting, dynamic people to lead their tours. Especially during the summer tourist season, these operators need extra tour escorts and leaders to handle the greater number of groups traveling. You can find out about becoming a tour guide by checking with large travel agencies who specialize in booking groups. You can call or write to tour operators directly. If you are fluent in one or more foreign languages and enjoy working with people, you already possess two of the most valuable assets for earning free travel as a tour leader.

TRAVEL FREE AS AN AIR COURIER

Have you ever seen ads in the classified travel section offering free travel as an air courier and wondered what they mean?

An *air courier* is someone who accompanies freight (often important documents) that has been checked as baggage on a flight. Air courier companies are businesses that promise very fast personal delivery of parcels being sent to a distant client. Air courier companies provide service to both domestic and foreign destinations. Some of the shipments are transported on commercial airlines; some go by private airplane. When using a commercial airline, the courier company usually puts a passenger on the flight and checks its shipment on the passenger's ticket. The shipment then becomes "passenger baggage" and always arrives at the destination at the same time as the air courier (or *on-board courier*).

Some courier companies use only their own employees as on-board couriers. Others offer courier assignments to the general public, in which case payment is made in the form of an exchange for free or deeply discounted (70 percent or more) air fare.

Here are some examples of recent round trip courier fares compared with regular coach and apex fares:

	Courier	**Coach**	**Apex**
NY-Paris	$350	$1,834	$ 548
NY-Frankfurt	$199	$2,234	$ 560
NY-London	$299	$1,972	$ 500
NY-Oslo	$199	$1,816	$ 630
NY-Rio de Jenerio	$499	$1,758	$1,133
NY-Caracus	$199	$ 976	$ 732
Los Angeles-Singapore	$425	$3,142	$1,283
Los Angeles-Tokyo	$350	$1,870	$1,117
Los Angeles-Hong Kong	$425	$2,380	$ 990
Los Angeles-Bangkok	$500	$2,760	$1,168

The key to becoming a courier is being flexible and able to travel within the timetable of the courier firm. The ticket can be for either one-way or round-trip travel, depending on company policy. Return portions for international trips are usually booked for one or two weeks after the original flight, but some courier companies offer a 30-day or open-ended ticket.

In some cases, "casual couriers" or freelancers are required to deposit $500 before booking a flight; the money is returned when the passenger returns. Other courier firms may charge a fee of $100 to $300, which is returned at the destination or upon return to the United States.

Air couriers accompany a variety of shipments including commercial paper (i.e., legal documents, tax documents), extremely perishable goods, or valuable objects, such as paintings, porcelain, or jewelry. Just recently my sister, who works for a museum in Los Angeles, traveled free to Egypt accompanying several important art pieces for an exhibit overseas. The art objects traveled in the seat next to her, and she got a free round-trip ticket to Paris and Cairo.

One of the main reasons for sending air couriers to foreign destinations is the fact that clearing customs is much faster for a package shipped as a passenger's baggage than one shipped alone as freight. In my sister's case, she actually had customs agents waiting for her at each stop ready to help speed up the generally slow customs process.

Working as a freelance air courier in exchange for free or very low air fare is a great travel opportunity requiring little or no skills. Air courier companies are using more freelancers (rather than their own staff) because of the cost-effective features to them: no salaries and no benefits are paid, and the courier company can recoup the money for the courier's ticket from its fee. There are also courier agents, companies that act as "procurement agencies" for courier companies that want to use nonstaff members as couriers but don't want the hassle of advertising, interviewing, qualifying, and scheduling them.

Because of the nature of courier flights as specialized "last-minute" travel, prices are in a constant state of flux. The following are courier services listed by originating cities:

COURIER SERVICES

Chicago

Tim Atkins (Booking agent for TNT Skypak of Chicago	(708) 453-7300

Los Angeles

IBC Pacific, Inc.	(213) 216-1637 or 641-2118
Jupiter Air	(213) 670-5251
Way To Go Travel, Inc.	(213) 851-2572
Midnight Express	(213) 672-1100
ANZ Travel (Australia New Zealand Travel)	(213) 379-2483

Miami

Intermail	(305) 433-8366

New York

Air Facilities	(718) 712-0630
Courier Travel Service, Inc.	(800) 922-2FLY
Halbart Express	(718) 656-8189
Intermail Courier	(718) 898-2526

continued. . .

| Now Voyager | (212) 431-1616 |
| Rush | (718) 439-9043 |

San Francisco

| Booking agent for TNT—Skypak | (415) 583-5074 |

MORE WAYS TO FLY FREE

Buy a new automobile overseas and the delivery company, dealer and/or factory will pay for your round-trip airfare. There are several companies specializing in European delivery that will arrange all necessary customs and vehicle inspections in this country. By arranging European delivery on a new Jaguar, BMW, Mercedes, Volvo, Saab, Porsche, Audi, Volkswagon, etc., you can save $4,000 to $7,000 on the price *and* get a free trip in the bargain.

Below are some examples of recent promotions by various airlines, hotels, etc., that offered free airfare when combined with other services:

- Pan Am offered a free ticket to any Pan Am destination in the continental United States, Bermuda, the Caribbean, or Mexico with completion of a Pan Am round-trip to Europe. Any type of published fare qualified, and the free ticket was for the same class as the qualifying ticket, coach/economy excursion to first class. Some restrictions and blackouts applied and the free ticket was not transferable.

- The Jamaica Hotel offered to pay one free air fare for two guests traveling together for a minimum of seven nights. The Hotel specializes in all-inclusive adult vacations with golf, snorkeling, scuba diving, sailing, catamaran cruises, bicycling and windsurfing among its activities. This was a package deal including room, meals, open bar and airport transfers.

- Hawaiian Airlines offered free round-trip tickets between Honolulu and its neighbor islands Kauai, Maui, Molokai, Lanai, or the Big Island to vacationers flying to the islands (from the mainland) on the airline. To sweeten the deal, they threw in a free car for each day a car was rented at regular rates from Dollar Rent-A-Car.

- Aston Hotels and Resorts in Hawaii offered guests who completed a four-night stay at their properties on Kauai, Oahu, Maui, or Hawaii, free interisland airfare. Guests received two one-way interisland tickets on Hawaiian Airlines or four one-way tickets if they stayed seven nights at one Aston Resort.

- Guests staying nine nights in any of the 39 USA Plus 91 hotels (Includes Intercontinental and Windham Hotels in North America) earned a free round-trip coach ticket on Pan Am, SAS, United or American tickets were valid for any destination in the continental United States, Hawaii, Europe, Canada or the Caribbean.

CHAPTER
4
HOW TO MAKE THE
AIRLINES PAY YOU:
**BUMPING, CANCELLING, OVERBOOKING, AND DELAYS
(OR HOW TO PROFIT FROM THE AIRLINES' MISTAKES)**

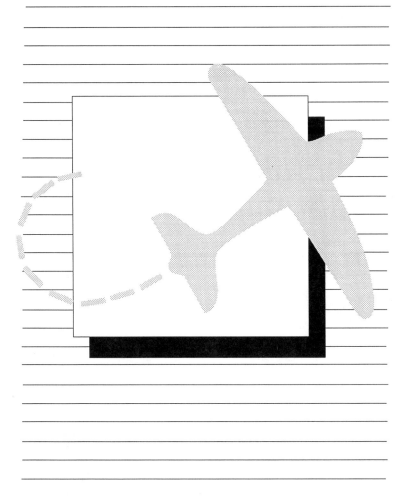

HOW TO MAKE THE AIRLINES PAY YOU:
BUMPING, CANCELLING, OVERBOOKING, AND DELAYS
(OR HOW TO PROFIT FROM THE AIRLINES' MISTAKES)

BUMPING

If you can get yourself bumped from an overbooked flight, you are entitled to receive a free flight voucher as compensation. In other words, this is the one case in which you can fly for free, compliments of the airlines, without having to pay them anything. Bumping is the airlines' alternative to compensating you in cash for taking you off a flight for which you have a confirmed reservation.

Bump tickets can be worth far more than the legally specified dollar compensation for overbooking. By offering these tickets, the airlines have nearly eliminated passenger complaints for overbooking. With the reward of a free ticket, enough people are usually willing to relinquish their confirmed space to accommodate other confirmed ticket holders who don't want to wait for another flight. You are put on the next available flight to your original destination and have a new ticket good for another trip at another time.

The chances of getting bumped on any given flight in the United States are slightly less than 1 out of 500, but if you are interested in obtaining a bump ticket, try airlines that allow travelers on crowded flights to volunteer for bumping—usually on a first-come, first-served basis—at the departure gate.

You can improve your odds for getting bumped by following a few guidelines:

- Choose the airline with the worst bumping record at the most congested airport. You can check the bumping record through the Department of Transportation's monthly *Air Traveler Consumer Report*. The most congested airport would be in a hub city through which an airline connects most of its longer city to city flights, thus eliminating non-stop flights to cities served by that airline. Because of the sheer volume of passengers passing through the larger hub airports, there is usually a great deal more congestion as well as flight delays occurring in the part of the airport used by the hub airline.

- Fly at the most popular, busiest times of the day for the route you are taking. This means, typically, Monday morning, Thursday and Friday afternoon/evening, or the beginning or end of a major holiday weekend.

- Bring only carry-on luggage with you.

- Arrive and check in early at the airport since some airlines require you to have checked in on time in order to qualify for a bump ticket.

- Once at the departure gate, immediately volunteer to be bumped in case of overbooking.

- You are more likely to get bumped during the summer at an airport with extreme heat or high altitude. Hot weather causes thinner air. With thinner air, airplanes need to fly lighter. That means less luggage and sometimes less passengers.

There are, of course, no guarantees that will assure you of a bump ticket. You need to weigh the inconvenience of rescheduling a trip with the reward of a free ticket. The airlines want to issue as few bump tickets as possible, so they try to estimate exactly how many no-shows will figure in their booking process.

When is a bump ticket most useful? When you have to travel on short notice and have only the choice of buying a full-fare ticket rather than an excursion one. With a bump ticket in hand, you are traveling at a much lower cost than full-fare coach purchased at the last minute.

Also, most bump tickets don't require a minimum advance purchase or a Saturday-night stay. In fact, a few only allow 24 or 48 hour advance reservations (which, obviously, wouldn't work in planning a trip very far in advance).

Bump tickets are very marketable. Since they have few restrictions they are often considered more valuable than a purchased coach/economy excursion worth as much as $400 to $500. Also bump tickets or vouchers are transferable to anyone, thus allowing coupon brokers to buy and sell them without breaking the airline rules.

WHAT YOU CAN GET WHEN YOU DON'T WANT A BUMP TICKET FOR OVERBOOKING

Since a confirmed reservation with an airline doesn't necessarily guarantee you a seat, what are you entitled to if you don't want a free flight with a bump ticket?

- You get to keep your original ticket and either use it on another flight or have it refunded.

- The airline is usually obligated under its conditions of contract (or carriage) to try to put you on the next available flight arriving at your destination at no cost to you.

- If they find another flight arriving at your destination within one hour of your original flight, you are not entitled to compensation.

- If the substitute flight arrives between one and two hours later, the airline must pay you the fare of your oversold flight (up to $200 maximum). If the flight they replace you on arrives more than two hours after your original flight, or if there is no other suitable flight, the airline must pay you twice your fare up to $400 maximum.

The law requires you to be paid on the spot (unless you are running to catch an alternative flight that is leaving right away. In that case, the airline must pay you within 24 hours). The airline may offer you a free bump ticket or a travel voucher, neither of which you need to accept in lieu of cash (although as we mentioned above, the travel voucher/bump tickets are usually worth significantly more than the money).

In addition, because of a recent court ruling, bumped passengers can now turn down the free tickets or refunds they are offered and sue the airline for damages. The amounts given above are the minimum required by Federal law for airlines to pay. The ruling stems from a suit filed by a Montana lawyer against Northwest Airlines. Essentially, he argued against the airline's right to sell passengers restricted tickets that cannot be exchanged or refunded, then turn around and bump those passengers because they overbooked a flight.

However, unhappy bumped passengers should bear in mind that there is no guarantee of recovery, and a lawsuit can drag on for a long time.

DELAYS AND CANCELLATIONS—WHAT YOU CAN DO ABOUT THEM

First of all, if an airline delays or cancels a flight and you miss an important meeting, you cannot successfully sue the airline. The "conditions of contract" that appears on the back of every ticket for a domestic flight are legally binding. They state that schedules are not binding on the airline. Once you hold the ticket, you must live with the rules written on the back regardless of whether you have read them or not.

Mechanical problems or delays due to weather may:

1. Force a cancellation.
2. Require an airline to substitute a smaller plane for the originally scheduled one.
3. Cause you to miss a connection.
4. Divert your flight to another airport.

If these occur the airline is legally bound to use its best efforts to get you to your destination either by resuming the original flight as soon as possible, putting you on its next flight with available seats (even if it means putting you in a higher class if your class is filled), or chartering a bus to your final destination.

That is about the extent to which an airline will go in rectifying delays and cancellations. However, in the case of a schedule irregularity, i.e., you're delayed at a connecting airport, diverted to an unscheduled airport for more than a few hours, or there was a change in the published schedule that you were not aware of, you may be entitled to some special compensation. This might include a meal or two, long distance phone calls to alert others at your destination, or a hotel room for an overnight delay.

Under most conditions of contract, if the airline cannot put you on an alternative flight, or puts you on a flight that is unacceptable to you, you can request a refund under the *involuntary refund* rules. But remember, under most of the conditions of contract, the alternative transportation offered has to be acceptable to you. In other words, the alternative has to be *so* unacceptable as to have caused a provable hardship or loss, in which case, even if your ticket is marked nonrefundable, you are entitled to a refund.

There is also the question of whether the alternative flight or transportation leaves or arrives so much later than your original flight that it is unacceptable, and you decide not to go ahead with any transportation arranged by the delaying/canceling airline. Again, you'd better have a very good reason for refusing the airline's offer and subsequently trying to obtain a refund. (More about this in the section on Refunds.)

A final word on delays. Before the introduction of Apex and MaxSaver fares, if a flight was canceled or delayed and the airline had no available alternative flights, you could use your regular ticket on another airline, without question. However, with today's restricted tickets, competing fares and short term cut-rate promotions, an airline does not have to "sign over" your original ticket to another airline. And even if it does, the other airline doesn't have to accept it if the value is below the fare charged for a ticket without advance purchase. Welcome to the world of air fare wars!

CHAPTER
5
OTHER WAYS TO
SAVE ON FLYING

OTHER WAYS TO SAVE ON FLYING

In addition to the discounts and bargains discussed in the previous chapters, including ways to fly for free, there are other nontraditional, creative routes to saving on air fare. These include alternative ticket sources such as consolidators and bucket shops. We also musn't forget the often confusing, but still rewarding frequent-flyer programs. Travel clubs (some of which were discussed in Chapter 2 in the section on Last-Minute Travel) are another way to save in all areas of travel.

Senior citizens earn a section of their own since the airlines, along with the other segments of the travel industry, have come to realize the huge potential in catering to the mature market. Air passes and round-the-world fares are opportunities for those who do a great deal of international traveling to buy their tickets in bulk, or several at one time. Finally, after sharing with you the knowledge and strategies that will help you cut the high cost of flying, we'll show you the many overlooked situations when "nonrefundable" tickets can become refundable.

TRAVEL CLUBS

Travel clubs, in general, offer members their most significant savings on hotel and condominium accommodations, cruises, car rentals, sightseeing, and entertainment. They also offer extra benefits such as travel insurance, emergency medical/legal assistance, "bargain hotlines" for last-minute travel updates, frequent-traveler programs, and periodic newsletters and magazines outlining their latest offers. Some even offer credit card privileges with extensive credit lines, which like most consumer credit cards, charge hefty interest rates on unpaid balances. The bigger discounts tend to be limited to times when airlines, hotels, or cruises don't expect to be full. Dues for travel clubs vary, but average $60 or less per family per year.

It is almost impossible to get a big discount on a domestic airline ticket through a members-only travel club. (See page 81 on Hideaways for the exception.) For international travel, you are better off buying your tickets through a ticket consolidator and use the travel club for the rest of your travel arrangements. However, some clubs do offer discounts on a limited range of consolidator airfares; so as always, check and compare prices before buying.

In addition to the discounts for their travel services, some travel clubs which basically function as cut-rate travel agents, also work on a rebate system. In this case, the agents arrange for a discount from their suppliers and in turn rebate some of their commission to their members, in effect discounting the "list" price. These rebates average between 4 and 8 percent of the cost of each trip a member takes through the club. The rebates can take the form of cash or credit toward free travel on future trips taken with the club. Clubs that offer rebates are competing with the very large discount travel clubs and booking services. Since their discounts tend to be somewhat more modest, they offer the added incentive of a rebate.

We advise you to choose a travel club that will give you big discounts, not small ones. In the end, you may be better off paying full commission to a club that's good at arranging big discounts from major suppliers than settling for a partial rebate of a small commission. But if you are planning on buying big-ticket service and can't get a big discount, a rebate may save you enough money to make up that difference.

As for saving on domestic fares Hideaways International, a Massachusetts-based travel club (800-843-4433), offers its members discounts on domestic airlines. The main benefit of using a club that offers travel discounts in the United States is for those who can't use low-cost coach excursions because of the advance purchase, Saturday night stay, or other restrictions. They also offer first class discounts to members.

Below are some agencies and travel clubs that own (or are associated with) agencies selling to dues-paying club members. These clubs offer cut rates on nearly every travel service and a few offer discounted last-minute travel.

Travel Clubs and Cut-Rate Travel Agencies	Telephone Number
Club Costa	(800) 225-0381
Cost Less Travel Bargain Center	(415) 397-6868
Discount Travel International	(800) 221-8139
First Travel	(312) 240-2626
Hideaways International	(800) 843-4433
McTravel Travel Service	(800) 333-3335
Mobil Plus	(800) 621-5581
Pennsylvania Travel	(800) 331-0947
Sears Discount Travel	(800) 433-9383
Stand-Buys	(800) 433-9383
Smart Traveller	(305) 448-3338
Travelers Advantage	(800) 548-1116
Travel Avenue	(800) 333-3335
Travel Brokers	(800) 999-8748

In addition to the travel clubs described above, hundreds of banks offer travel-agency services (some even offer rebates) with their MasterCard® and Visa® cards. In a highly competitive industry, these services are one way banks try to attract customers and build loyalty. Some include travel service with their ordinary cards; others limit it to "premium" or extra-fee versions. American Express and Diners Club also offer their cardholders a wide array of travel services.

THE CHEAPEST WAY TO
GET OUT OF THE COUNTRY:
CONSOLIDATORS AND BUCKET SHOPS

Consolidators are independent discount travel brokers who sell tickets directly to the public or travel agencies, or both. Consolidators obtain their tickets through international airlines that sell their surplus seats on a reward system for large volume and block purchases.

Under the Federal Aviation Act, although it is technically illegal for consolidators (a.k.a. bucket shops overseas) to sell you discounted airline tickets, it is not illegal for you to buy them. Some pressure has been taken off the consolidator's, however, since the Department of Transportation indicated that it would prosecute violators *only* when there was clear evidence that discounting had adversely affected a substantial number of persons and then only when accompanied by some other form of illegal or deceptive activity.

Consolidator fares are significantly lower than those you could purchase from low-fare specialists (the ones who have been complaining to DOT about the risks and illegal dealings of consolidators) who deal primarily with official published fares (even lower than the lowest Apex fares). Also they generally do not have the requirements and restrictions for advance bookings, minimum and maximum stay-over's. Tickets are available during holiday seasons (although in limited supply) as well as all other times during the year. Additionally, it is possible to purchase one-way tickets for about half the price of an airline's economy ticket, which usually requires a round-trip purchase. Although savings are often between $200 to $300 per ticket, always check current promotional fares if your goal is to find the absolute lowest possible fare.

Consolidators are usually located in large metropolitan areas. They advertise their extraordinary low international (and some domestic) fares in the travel section of the newspapers. You can also find them in the classified section of *USA Today*. Sometimes an airline will give you the name of its consolidator, especially those servicing Third World countries. We advise you do a lot of shopping around before buying, ticket availability and prices vary.

Some people are wary of using a consolidator rather than a retail travel agent for several reasons including:

- Consolidator tickets are often for less-than-direct routes. They originate only from gateway cities so you have to arrange getting to the gateway city separately.

- There may be stiff penalties for canceling or missing the flight. Also if you miss the flight the tickets are usually good only on the issuing airline and only for the flight for which they were issued.

- Most of the time you are unable to pick the airline, flight time or specific route to your final destination. Sometimes, especially during peak periods, there are a limited number of consolidator tickets available.

- Consolidators are not regulated and some operate using unethical or unsound methods. As we mentioned in our discussion of coupon brokers (who sometimes are also consolidators), always pay for your tickets with a credit card to insure protection of your purchase.

- Consolidators are often reluctant to name their airlines, simply promising a major scheduled carrier. This is because the airlines fear naming them could undermine their fare structures.

Here is a sampling of some consolidator/bucket shops by state:

CONSOLIDATOR/BUCKET SHOPS

California

Allied Travel Center	(213) 410-1141
Air Kit	(213) 482-8778
Air Services	(213) 854-8570
British European Travel	(800) 747-1476
C and H	(213) 387-2288
Canatours	(213) 223-1111
Council Travel	(213) 208-3551
Jetway	(800) 421-8771
Bargain Air	(213) 377-2919
Euro-Asia Express	(800) 782-9625
CL Thomson Express	(415) 398-2535
Char-Tours	(800) 323-4444
Planewrap Tours	(818) 989-1187
Sunbeam	(213) 483-8363
Sunline Express	(800) 877-2111
ANZ Travel	(800) 525-8397
Cheap Tickets	(800) 234-4522

continued...

Florida

International Travel Club	(800) 248-2582
Interworld Miami	(800) 331-4456
Travel Leaders	(800) 432-4343
Coral Gables	(800) 323-3218
25 Travel Inc.	(800) 252-5052

Illinois

Hudson Holiday	(800) 323-6855
Interpacific	(312) 853-2700
McTravel	(800) 333-3335
Mena	(312) 472-5631
Overseas Express	(312) 262-4971
Union Express	(312) 565-0125

Maryland

Old Country	(800) 386-2743

Minnesota

ITA Eagan	(800) 482-8747

Missouri

Unitravel	(800) 325-2222

New York

Access International	(212) 333-7280
Airlink Travel	(212) 867-7770

continued...

Ameropa	(718) 522-1000
Council Charter	(800) 223-7402
Destinations Unlimited	(212) 980-8220
Maharaja Travel	(800) 223-6862
Wholesale	(800) 223-6862
TFI Tours	(800) 727-6606

Travac (offices in New York,
  (Los Angeles, San Francisco,and
  Orlando)
	(800) 872-8800

Up & Away Travel	(800) 876-2929

Ohio

Tailor Made	(513) 791-2784

Oregon

Pacific Gateway	(503) 294-6478
STT Worldwide	(503) 641-8866

Pennsylvania

HTI	(215) 629-9997

Texas

Airvalue	(800) 527-8448 (800) 482-8282
Katty Van Houston	(800) 528-9826

Virginia

Fellowship	(800) 446-7667
Trans Am	(800) 822-7600

continued...

Washington

ATBI	(206) 771-2527
Marco Polo	(206) 621-0700
Pacific Gateway	(206) 624-2228
Sun Makers	(800) 841-4321

(if a consolidator listed is in your area, call information for the local number).

In a recent development several airlines including Pan Am, British Airways, Delta, and TWA, have announced special fares designed to compete with consolidator prices. For example, a New York—Frankfurt round-trip fare was advertised at $348, while a Los Angeles, San Francisco, or Seattle trip to Frankfurt cost $488. Round-trip fares to London from Detroit, Miami, New York, and Washington cost $298 and from the West, $438.

However, these fares have an unusually long advance purchase requirement of 45 days, and other minimum/maximum restrictions. They are also nonrefundable. Even though the fares are exceptional, if you can't plan your trip 45 days in advance, you'll probably do better looking for comparative consolidator fares without the restrictions.

In an unusual move, TWA recently added some important limits and restrictions to its consolidator tickets in addition to the normal ones. These included:

No change in itinerary by the passenger.

No transfers to another airline.

Refund only given through the issuing travel agency (if given at all).

No advance seat assignment.

No special meal requests.

No frequent-flyer credit.

No compensation for accommodations or meals in case of a delay or missed connection.

Tickets are not allowed to be used by anyone under 18 unless accompanied by an adult.

TWA is currently the only airline labeling its tickets with specific restrictions. However, we strongly suggest you learn about *all* restrictions on consolidator as well as airlines' special promotion tickets *before* purchasing them.

A final word on consolidators. Many are now offering discounts on hotel and resort accommodations, especially chain operations. Check when making your airline arrangements for additional discounts on these services.

SENIOR CITIZEN DISCOUNTS

We've included a separate section for senior citizen discounts for a couple of reasons. First, there are a wide variety of programs and fares available just for seniors. Second, since many people take advantage of their retirement years by traveling (using some of their nest egg or investments), we see no reason why they, too, shouldn't save money just because they finally have it to enjoy. The more you save, the more traveling you can do in the future.

There are four ways airlines currently attract mature travelers:

1. Clubs with discounts (frequent-flyers).
2. Straight clubs.
3. Unlimited mileage passes.

4. Coupon books.

Keep in mind that most ticket agents do not ask the ages of adults flying, so you have to volunteer your age and ask what kinds of senior fares are available. Don't assume that all fares start at 62 or 65 years. Some savings are offered starting at 50 and up (for example, those in conjunction with proof of membership in the American Association of Retired Persons [AARP]) and vary considerably from airline to airline. Most programs allow a companion of any age, regardless of sex or relationship to travel at the same reduced fare.

Most airlines offer a 10 percent senior citizen discount off regular fares on all flights. In addition to the regular discount, as a senior you can pay even less by booking a MaxSaver/excursion fare, flying at night or using other discounts, enabling them to take advantage of a double discount. The more flexible you are in your plans, the more choices you have for saving money. As always, ask your travel agent or airline reservationist for the lowest current fare and compare it with your senior discount fare.

Several airline travel clubs (including American, Continental, Northwest, TWA, United, and USAir) offer special programs for seniors over 62. Lifetime membership fees range between $500 and $700 and $200 and $300 for spouses. Amenities include use of private clubs in airports, plus services such as check cashing, copiers, fax machines, beverage bars (some with free cocktails), personal computers, periodicals, conference rooms, free local calls, airline, hotels and car rental reservations.

For example, United Airlines offers the "Silver Wings Plus" program for adults 62 or over. Travelers receive a 10 percent discount on United and United Express fares to the United States, Mexico, Singapore, Thailand, Korea, Taiwan, Hong Kong, China, Australia, New Zealand, West Germany, France, Canada, and the Philippines. The program is also good on Alitalia, Sabena, British Airways, Iberia, and KLM. Members receive discounts from 10 to 50 percent at several participating chain hotels and resorts as well, discounts on Hertz, Alamo, and Dollar rental cars, and a quarterly travel magazine. Membership costs $50 and includes a $50 discount certificate. A "Companion Membership" for another person, regardless of age, costs an additional $100. (Seniors 60 years and over can join the club for $25 and receive hotel and car rental discounts and the *Silver Wings Plus* travel magazine.)

Some of the most attractive deals for seniors are the coupon packages offered by several airlines for seniors 62 and over. These are especially designed for those who plan to do a lot of traveling over a year. Coupons are sold in books of four or eight. Each coupon is good for a one-way domestic flight between any two points served by the airline within the contiguous United States, Hawaii, Alaska, the U.S. Virgin Islands, and Puerto Rico. Travel to Alaska or Hawaii usually requires two coupons. Currently Alaska, America West, TWA, Continental, Northwest, American, Delta, United, and USAir offer senior coupon programs. Prices range from $396 to 473 for books of four one-way coupons, and from $720 to $790 for books of eight one-way coupons. Coupons are valid for one year from the purchase date and earn frequent-flyer credit. Check restrictions and requirements before flying to make sure you can qualify for using your senior coupons.

Instead of using coupons, Southwest Airlines offers senior fares ranging from $19 to $79 one-way, which are good on any published Southwest Airlines' route. Adults 65 and over qualify for these special fares, with no advance purchase required.

Some airlines are rewarding seniors as they get older. For instance, a senior citizen between 62 and 70 saves 70 percent off regular coach fares; up to age 99 they get a percentage discount matching their age, and if they can prove they are 100 years old, they fly free in first class!

For seniors who really like to travel, Continental offers two "passport" programs with a single, annual, upfront payment. The first, the coach class "Freedom Passport" allows travelers 62 and over to take a one-way trip each week for a year, or 23 round trips, anywhere in the continental United States for $1,599 (first class, $1,999). Any one city can be visited up to three times. A companion option, also $1,599, allows a traveler of any age to accompany a qualifying senior on the same itinerary. The "Global Passport" for seniors sells for $2,999 (first class, $4,999) and allows up to three trips to destinations in Canada, Central America, and Mexico, and one trip each to Hawaii, Europe, and the South Pacific.

Foreign airlines also offer discounts for seniors. These include:

Mexicana: 10 percent discount for seniors 62 or older on international travel from the United States to Mexico and domestic travel within Mexico.

British Airways: "Privileged Traveller" program for adults 60 years and over. Members receive 10 percent discount on all airfares at all times, plus 10 percent on London Plus holiday programs, select orient express departures, select Cunard Line Cruises, and special senior Apex air fares.

El Al Israel Airlines: Fifteen percent senior citizen discount for 60 years and over.

Alitalia: Members of United's Silver Wings Plus travel club who are over 65 receive 10 percent discount on all flights.

Iberia: Members of United's Silver Wings Plus travel club receive 10 percent discount off any published fare.

Other foreign airlines offering senior fares include: Lot Polish Airlines, Tap Air Portugal, SAS, Finnair, KLM Royal Dutch Airlines, Lufthansa, Sabena and Yugoslav Airlines.

AIR PASSES: FLY MORE, PAY LESS

There are special air fare deals that make it easier and sometimes cheaper to travel to individual countries and multi-country regions. They fall into three categories:

1. Flat-cost passes that allow you to take an unlimited number of trips at a fixed price for a set period. Repeat visits to a city are often restricted.

2. Set-price tickets or visitor tickets that give you a certain number of individual one-way flights for a set price or a fixed price per flight for as many flights as you want. Again, repeat visits to a city are often restricted.

3. Discount coupons that give you a set discount or reduction from regular airfare purchased one ticket at a time.

The airlines sometimes are reluctant to work with travelers on putting together these special deals. Often the reservation clerks don't even know about them. You need to ask about them.

Domestic programs are sometimes limited to certain groups such as students or seniors. Sometimes they are sold as part of promotions between the airlines and travel clubs. For international passes, these programs are usually open to persons residing outside the country or countries within which the flights are being taken.

United States airlines offer similar programs for domestic United States flights to persons living abroad even if those persons are United States citizens. Some United States residents, as a result, have enrolled in these programs while out of the country, used a foreign address and then used the passes, tickets, or coupons in the United States.

A variety of regional and national fares provide extended air travel at special rates. Because of changing economic conditions, fuel prices, etc., these fares and their restrictions change periodically. New programs come and go, so always check current fares for programs offered by the domestic airline (or airlines) of the country(ies) where you are planning to travel.

The following sections list examples of air passes, visitor tickets, and discount coupons offered to travelers by foreign airlines.

Travel to Asia/Pacific

AUSTRALIA
Ansett Air and East-West have "See Australia" visitor discount programs with 25 percent reductions on economy travel. Qantas offers "Discover Australia," with 45 percent reduction on some domestic routes. East-West also offers regional "airpass" options and visitor tickets. Australian Airlines has special fares for 8 air passes for travel within the country. Check restrictions and current availability.

CIRCLE PACIFIC
With the greatly increased travel between Asian/Pacific destinations, many airline combinations for special fares have been offered concurrently allowing travelers to circle the Pacific basin. There are usually restrictions for advance purchase, but most tickets are good for six months or more. Travel either clockwise or counterclockwise. Once travel has started, you need to continue in the same direction. Most Circle Pacific tickets permit only four stops at the basis fare.

Circle Pacific fares are expensive, with economy fares about as high as round-the-world fares; first class fares are higher. Check consolidator prices to compare their equivalent trips with multiple stops.

INDIA
Recently Indian Air offered a 21-day "Discover India" pass, which allows unlimited flights throughout the country for $400. There is also a regional 7-day "India Wonderfare" pass, one for each of four regions. Each pass is priced at $200 and allows unlimited

travel within its region. Both the national and regional passes do not allow return to any city you've already flown to unless it's for a connecting flight. You have a year from the date of purchase in which to begin using the passes, which are all on a consecutive-day basis.

NEW ZEALAND
The "Freedom Pass" visitor ticket books provide coupons good for a one-way domestic economy flight on Air New Zealand, or Mt. Cook Airlines.

POLYNESIA
Polynesia Airways, the national airline of Western Samoa, offers the "PolyPass," valid for 30 days, providing unlimited travel over its South Pacific routes. This is a good value for extended island hopping, especially if you can also use it in place of separate round-trip from Auckland or Sidney. Ticket is nonrefundable once travel has begun.

Travel to Europe

FINLAND
The "Holiday Ticket" pass, valid for 15 days, provides unlimited economy travel on domestic Finnair routes. A "Fly and Drive" visitor discount program valid for 15 days, provides 50 percent reduction on domestic round-trip and open-jaw airfares on designated off-peak flights.

FRANCE
The "Le France" pass provides unlimited economy air travel on Air Inter in France on any seven days of a month. Flights serve 28 cities. There are blackouts on a few peak period flights.

SCANDINAVIA

During the summer months, "Visit Scandinavia" passes are offered for travel in July and August, with up to five economy flights
within Denmark, Norway, and Sweden. The pass is valid for up
to 30 days after arrival in Scandinavia and can be used inter-
changeably on the three Scandinavian airlines, Danair, Linjeflyg,
and SAS.

SPAIN

The "Visit Spain" pass is valid for 60 days and provides visits to
over 30 destinations on Spain's mainland, the Balearic Islands,
and Spanish Morocco served by Iberia or its domestic affiliate,
Aviaco. This is a good value for travelers heading for more than
one remote area, especially the islands. Multiple visits are per-
mitted for connecting flights.

UNITED KINGDOM

The "Visit UK" ticket is valid for 30 days and provides individual
domestic economy flights among all cities served by Dan-Air:
Aberdeen, Belfast, Bradford, Bristol, Cardiff, Inverness, Jersey,
Leeds, London, and Newcastle. This is a good value for reaching
Belfast or Scottish cities.

Travel to Latin America

ARGENTINA

The "Visit Argentina " pass provides unlimited Economy air travel
in Argentina for 30 days. "Visit Argentina" visitor tickets allows
stops at any three cities in Argentina for 14 days. These are
offered by all three Argentine airlines operating domestic flights:
Aerolineas Argentines, Austral Lineas Aereas, and LADE. Check
restrictions. This is generally a good value even if you are visiting
only a few cities.

BOLIVIA

The "Visit Bolivia" pass is valid for 28 days and provides travel among major Bolivian cities served by Lloyd Aereo Boliviano (LAB). Generally speaking, traveling by air offers somewhat more safety and security than traveling by surface in this remote country.

BRAZIL

The "Brazil Airpass" is offered at comparable prices by Trans Brasil, Varig, and VASP, Brazil's major airlines. Passes provide unlimited domestic economy travel for up to 21 days. Check for restrictions.

CHILE

"Visit Chile" fare on LanChili has four options with varying stopovers (economy only) valid for 21 days. Chili's other airline, Ladeco, also offers a "Visit Chili" 21 day pass providing stopovers in up to 12 mainland cities. These are a good value if you want to explore this large country, but for visiting just the lake country, a Santiago-Puerto Montt round-trip is less expensive. Check current prices and compare.

COLUMBIA

The "Know Columbia" visitor ticket valid for 30 days, provides 10 stopovers anywhere in Columbia served by Avianca, except Leticia and San Andres Island.

MEXICO

"Vimex" visitor discount program provides 25 percent reductions on domestic Mexican flights to travelers who use Mexicana round-trip from outside the country.

PERU

AeroPeru and Faucett both offer "Visit Peru" passes, valid for 30 days for unlimited economy travel within Peru. All flights must be on the same airlines.

VENEZUELA
The "Airpass" provides unlimited domestic economy travel on Avensa. No limit on stopovers in any city. For just one side trip, an individual ticket may be cheaper. For more extensive travel, the pass is a good buy, especially compared with the often primitive modes of surface transportation.

South American Passes

All three multi-country South American passes cost less than all but the most restricted economy excursions from the United States to main cities of southern South America, Buenos Aires, Rio, Santiago:

> AeroPeru, Peru's national airline, offers "Visit South America" pass valid for 45 days, for round-trip travel from the United States to any South American city it serves.

> Lineas Aereas Paraguayas (LAP), Paraguay's national airline, offers "Visit South America" pass valid for 30 days, for round trip travel from the United States to any South American city it serves.

> Avianca, Columbia's national airline, offers YIT21 visitor tickets valid for 7 to 21 days for round-trip travel from the United States to any five of the South American cities it serves.

Canada

The "Atlantic Canadapass" provides reduced price air travel among 16 cities in Canada's four Atlantic provinces. The pass is attractive if you want to enjoy these scenic provinces. Flights can be booked on either Air Canada or Air Nova, a regional airline. Check for restrictions.

To determine your best cost options, always compare the price of an air pass, visitor ticket, or visitor discount fare with whatever alternatives are available. Fare prices to inquire about might include: a single long-haul ticket that includes all the stops you want to make, side trips by surface transportation (rental car or train), or airline side trips purchased individually.

An example of a current domestic airlines promotion is TWA's "Takeoff Pass," which offers six low-cost, round-trip coach/economy flights in a year, but does not earn you frequent-flyer credit. The "Takeoff Pass" provides three round-trip tickets within the continental United States, one to the Bahamas or Puerto Rico, one to Europe, and one to Hawaii. You can substitute an additional continental United States round trip for any one of the Bahamas/Puerto Rico, Europe, or Hawaii trips. There is no limit on the number of times you can visit any one city (other than the limit on total flights, so you can use all the United States round trips on the same route. The European trip allows one en-route stopover in Europe in addition to the final destination.

The cost of the pass is $1,995, and it appears to be a good buy if used for long trips (compared with the cost of separately purchased tickets for the same travel). However, if you consider frequent-flyer mileage, which could earn a West Coast traveler close to 40,000 miles of frequent-flier credits for the trip, the value becomes a lot less apparent. At an estimated value of $.02/mile, this credit would be worth $800. Refiguring for mileage, the cost of the "Takeoff Pass" becomes close to the cheapest available separate tickets for the maximum amount of travel possible taken with the pass.

There are several restrictions on using the pass, as well as the fact that you are paying up front for a great deal of future travel. One positive aspect of the pass is that it gives travelers the option of choosing between tickets that include frequent-flyer credit and cheaper tickets that don't. Those who would benefit most from the "Takeoff Pass" are frequent travelers who can plan trips a week ahead but can't accept the Saturday-night restriction on the cheapest excursion fares.

Pan Am's version of an air pass is its "Value Pass." Purchasers of this program are allowed four round trip flight—one each to Europe, Latin America, or Hawaii, the Caribbean or Mexico, and two to any city in the continental United States served by Pan Am. The pass costs approximately $1,000 (it was not being sold at the time of this writing) and is offered during off-season travel times. This is a good value if you are planning your travels during nonpeak times.

United Airlines has introduced the "Pass Plus" program, aimed at frequent business travelers. Under the program travelers purchase travel passes for periods ranging from two years to life. The passes start at $16,000 for two years of travel up to 25,000 miles each year and go up to unlimited travel for the life of the passholder and a companion. Again, this is a lot of money to part with up front, so consider the investment in this program and your future travel plans carefully before going for it.

AROUND-THE-WORLD FARES

If you are planning to make stops at several widely spread destinations on a long international journey, you might check into an around-the-world fare, which includes several stops for one price over a length of time (usually six months). The various American and foreign airlines have worked out joint agreements allowing travelers to use their airlines for a single trip without having to buy separate tickets for each leg. Generally you can make unlimited stops in the destinations served by an airline, but you are allowed only one stop in each city. All travel must be in one direction only: east to west or west to east. No backtracking to a city that is past where you have already been.

Around-the-world fares can represent significant savings for those traveling business or first class. There are also savings for coach class fares. Fares range from $2,000 to $3,000, depending on the number of stopovers and which area of the world you are circling. The airlines have constructed more than 70 different international itineraries to choose from around the world (excepting African and South American itineraries, which are difficult to find).

A recent example of around-the-world fares is TWA's special "Round the World" programs, available for as low as $1,899. The fare combines travel on six other airlines: Japan Airlines, Malaysia Airlines, Korea Air, Singapore Airlines, Qantas, and Cathay Pacific. Travelers can visit Europe, the Middle East, Asia, the Pacific, Australia, and the United States. Advance booking of 14 to 21 days is required and travel must continue in one direction around the world.

FREQUENT-FLYER PROGRAMS

In 1981 American Airlines introduced the first frequent-flyer program, the AAdvantage program. Since that time the frequent-flyer program concept has been adopted by practically every major domestic airline, some smaller regional airlines, and many international carriers acting as partners with the domestics. The programs have been expanded, overhauled, changed, cut-back, added-to, used, abused, and turned inside out to where most members scarcely know from day to day what their rights and privileges are for their hard earned mileage points. They change so often that any attempt to delineate individual airline programs would be outdated by the time this book goes to press. Instead, we will give you program highlights, advantages and disadvantages and a few examples of recent special offers for members of frequent-flyer clubs.

Under a frequent-flyer program, a passenger can a accumulate/earn points for flying on the airline. Points are redeemed in the form of travel awards for free travel-class upgrades and free tickets to select destinations flown by the airline or one of its partner airlines. (However, upgrading a ticket to a better class doesn't actually qualify as a money-saving reward, as many upgrades are given on full-fare economy tickets only. Since you can easily save 40 percent or more on the price of a full-fare economy ticket, using a "free" upgrade can actually cost you money.)

The programs were first conceived as a way to build passenger loyalty among business travelers, the largest class of flyers. Theoretically, nonbusiness travelers did not earn enough credit or mileage during a year to obtain worthwhile awards. However, if a person who earned the credit while traveling for business passes the award to someone who does not have the opportunity to travel for business, then those nonfrequent flyers can also take advantage of the savings and upgrades from these programs.

Building brand loyalty among the nation's business travelers worked for awhile, until travelers stopped going to great lengths to stay with one airline to earn mileage and joined the frequent-flyer clubs of all the other airlines they flew with. This allowed them to get the scheduling they wanted and still earn credit.

As a result, what the airline industry created in 1981 has turned into something of an unstoppable, consuming monster that refuses to stop growing and gobbling up more and more of what the airlines like to keep: profits. The frequent-flyer programs became so popular that they began cutting into the airline's coffers.

The airlines have responded to the unprecedented demand for free tickets and free upgrades by branching out into new areas of giving and earning awards. Their hope is that these new rewards will take the pressure off of giving away valuable seats. New ways to use mileage include:

- Free and discounted hotel rooms.
- Free and discounted car rentals.
- Free or deeply discounted companion tickets.
- Free car rental upgrades.

- Discounts on buying new cars.

- "Auctions" where members bid mileage points for different items.

- Free membership and services in private airline clubs.

- Free and discounted rooms on luxury cruise ships.

- Discounts on clothing, savings bonds, and a variety of consumer products.

Awarding these types of goods and services is an effective way for airlines to get accumulated mileage off their books.

New ways to earn mileage credit, in addition to the original concept of flying, include using designated hotels, credit cards, long-distance telephone companies, travel agencies, airport buses, car rental agencies, and purchases from certain retail stores.

Not long after the first frequent-flyer programs were introduced, a new industry was born: coupon brokering. This is where a frequent-flyer who has amassed more mileage than he could possibly ever use or give away to family or friends, sells (illegally, according to the airlines) his awards to a broker. The broker then sells them to consumers (who are usually less-frequent business travelers or vacationers), who buy the tickets at a price lower than the current published price. Some people also buy awards to use as free upgrades or because they carry fewer restrictions than excursion tickets. (See section on coupon brokers in Chapter 2.)

In addition to new and innovative ways of working off those millions of miles, airlines simply keep changing the rules of the programs to insure they give away as few of their precious seats as possible in order to keep more of their profits. These include:

- Increased "blackout dates" to where you need a calendar to mark all the times awards are invalid (they no longer cluster them only around major holidays).

- Doubled mileage requirements for certain first-class trips and trips that combine free tickets and free upgrades for companions who pay coach fare.

- Allocating fewer free-trip seats on popular flights to frequent-flyer award users.

To further confuse matters, with the increase in blackout periods and free-trip seat quotas often filling seat space up months in advance, some airlines are now allowing passengers to get around these restrictions by giving up some of their points. In other words, they're bribing their members to give up awards to break their own rules.

Some scheming flyers who covet first-class upgrades (which many airlines won't let them reserve more than 24 hours in advance to insure as many "paying" first-class travelers as possible), are booking phantom travelers in first-class seats. When the seat goes unclaimed at the airport, the frequent flyer, standing by with his award in his hand, steps forward and claims his first-class seat. The frequent flyer also has the option of canceling his phantom reservation less than 24 hours before the flight, then immediately calling back and upgrading his own ticket taking the canceled space.

There are, however, certain times of the year and certain situations in which airlines need and eagerly reward their frequent-flyer members. To spur travel during slow winter months, several airlines recently offered free tickets to travelers who took a certain number of trips during a specific time period. For example, Continental awarded free companion tickets to members of their OnePass program who made two round trips by a certain date. America West inaugurated its nonstop 747 New York–Las Vegas or Phoenix service by offering members of its FlightFund program free round-trip tickets to any America West destination after connecting through these cities to any California destination. In a special winter promotion most airlines rewarded their flyers who took 3 round-trips or 8 segments with a free round-trip ticket to any city within the continental United States,

Mexico, Canada, the Caribbean or Bermuda. Additional round trips earned a second free ticket. In some cases (Alaska, Pan Am and United) travelers received mileage in place of a free ticket. To qualify for the tickets, travelers had to join the airlines' frequent-flyer programs and pay at least $98 for the other trips.

Similarly, TWA'S frequent-flyer program introduced "The Corporate Blitz" offer. Members flying two round trips valued at $200 each earned a free companion ticket to any TWA destination (except Cairo and Tel Aviv). Travel was valid to Hawaii, the U.S.A., San Juan, or Europe.

Also, whereas most carriers a few years ago required at least 50,000 miles in order to be eligible for a free round-trip coach ticket anywhere in the 48 contiguous states, most have reduced that requirement to 20,000 miles of regular fare travel.

In a final effort to reward and maintain customer loyalty eroded by membership in multiple programs, the airlines are offering special perks to the most frequent of frequent-flyers. Known as "elite" programs, members are bumped up to a new, exclusive level of membership that often makes it easier to attain free trips by lowering redemption levels and giving mileage bonuses. There are also services like priority checking, wait-listing, baggage handling, free drinks, and use of the airline club. Some waive blackout periods and other restrictions for "elite" members. The well-publicized auctions that American Airlines held in Dallas and New York offering prizes ranging from use of an Avis Cadillac for a year to a deluxe trip to the 1990 Super Bowl, illustrate to what levels airlines will go to keep their best customers.

One possible glitch many frequent-flyers fear that may crop up in the future, is the Internal Revenue Service initiating rulings on awards as taxable income to the recipient. Although the IRS has been monitoring frequent-flyer programs, up to now it has not issued any regulations on the matter or indicated that an imminent announcement is on the horizon.

As you can see, it is nearly impossible for members to keep up with changes in frequent-flyer programs. However, they can subscribe to one of the monthly periodicals, such as *Business Flyer* or *Frequent Flyer*, which are devoted to reporting new frequent-flyer promotions and developments. Or they can buy travel magazines or subscribe to travel bulletins and newsletters that feature updates on frequent-flyer programs. Sometimes the travel section of a newspaper will have a periodic round-up on program changes.

Our advice is that if you're entitled to an award and there's a trip you want to take, redeem your credit and take the trip as soon as possible before the airline changes its and award requirements.

Listed below are airline frequent-flyer clubs and their toll-free phone numbers:

FREQUENT FLYER CLUBS

Frequent-Flyer Club	Telephone Number
Air Canada: Aeroplan	(800) 361-8253
Alaska: Gold Coast Travel	(800) 654-5669
America West: Fly Fund	(800) 247-5692
American: AAdvantage	(800) 433-7300
Braniff: Get-It-All Frequent Flier	(800) 346-8108
Continental: One Pass	(800) 525-0280
Delta: Frequent Flier	(800) 323-2323
Midway: Flyers First	(800) 621-5700
Midwest Express: Frequent Flyer	(414) 747-4646
Northwest: Work Perks	(800) 435-9696
Pan Am: World Pass	(800) 348-800
TWA: Frequent Flier Bonus	(800) 325-48150

continued. . .

| **United**: Mileage Plus | (800) 421-4655 |
| **USAir**: Frequent Traveler | (800) 872-4738 |

We recommend you enroll yourself and your family (it's free) in all of these programs, both to be ready to take advantage of mileage rewards and to be eligible for program bonuses and offers as they occur.

REFUNDS FOR "NONREFUNDABLE" TICKETS

Contrary to airline proclamations, there are ways to escape the dreaded "nonrefundable" rule that applies to most super-low-price or special-promotion excursion tickets. For example:

- If your flight is canceled for whatever reason or the airline is responsible for you missing your flight, the conditions of carriage require the airlines give you a full refund.

- If you miss your flight because of an illness or death in your immediate family, and you present written proof from a doctor or funeral director, most airlines allow you to use the ticket for a later flight going to the same destination. In many cases, if you decide not to reschedule your flight at all, you can get a full refund for your ticket with the proper certification.

- If you are called for jury duty or are subpoenaed, some airlines will allow you to cancel your flight (though they prefer you to reschedule at a later time) and will give you a refund.

- If you miss your flight completely because of an unexpected, unavoidable delay (i.e., extremely heavy airport traffic due to construction, an accident, etc.), some airlines will let you use your nonrefundable ticket for a standby flight on their airline to the same place as the original ticket.

- If you buy a discount airline ticket that carries a cancellation penalty, you can obtain a partial refund (minus the cancellation fee) plus 8 percent airline ticket tax due the IRS on each domestic ticket used. If the ticket is not used, then the tax is not due. However, in the past, airlines included the tax in the calculation of the cancellation penalty and therefore refunded less to the customer than was due. The IRS should have received its portion of the refund (the whole tax) but instead, some airlines kept the entire amount including the 8 percent windfall. Due to rulings on several class action suits going back to 1985, any part of the 8 percent tax must be turned over to the IRS. However, class action suits have not been brought against all of the airlines, and some continue to base the cancellation penalty on the full price of the ticket (including the tax), cheating the customer out of part of his refund. On a nonrefundable ticket, it is up to the ticket holder to demand a refund of the 8 percent.

- If you possess a nonrefundable, restricted ticket, many airlines will allow you to use your ticket for an earlier flight to the same destination on a standby basis (although this bends their rules). By checking the available seats on the earlier flights, you can usually tell what your chances are for getting on.

- If a ticket is not totally refundable, some airlines will endorse the ticket, allowing you to take a flight on another airline after you have paid the cancellation penalties. If missing your flight was the airline's fault, they should endorse your restricted ticket for use on another airline (with no penalties) if they cannot provide an adequate alternate flight.

- If you are bumped from a flight because it is overbooked and are holding a nonrefundable ticket, you can sue the airline for damages if you are not satisfied with the refund or free ticket they offer you.

- If you don't want to gamble on something going wrong, you can purchase "trip cancellation insurance," which protects you in case your flight is canceled.

- In the case of a national emergency, such as the recent Gulf War, most airlines loosened their restrictions on flights, giving credit to fliers afraid to fly because of terrorist threats. Vouchers were valid for travel up to a year after being issued.

- If you need to cancel a nonrefundable ticket on Wednesday through Monday, your "friendly" travel agent could void the ticket without a penalty since most agencies pay for tickets only once a week—on Tuesdays.

- Finally, for a fee, some airlines will allow you to change the return flight on a nonrefundable ticket. You still cannot get a refund or change destinations or routes, but what you get is a bit of flexibility in your plan should you need to make a change.

APPENDIX
I
DOMESTIC AND FOREIGN AIRLINES AND THEIR TOLL-FREE NUMBERS

APPENDIX I
DOMESTIC AND FOREIGN AIRLINES
AND THEIR TOLL-FREE NUMBERS

Domestic Airlines	Code	(800) Number
Alaska	AS	(800) 426-0333
Allegheny Commuter	US	(800) 428-4253
Aloha Airlines	AQ	(800) 367-5250
Alpha Air	7V	(800) 824-2610
America West Airlines	HP	(800) 247-5692
American Airlines	AA	(800) 433-7300
American Eagle	AA	(800) 433-7300
Continental Airlines	CO	(800) 525-0280
Delta Air Lines	DL	(800) 221-1212
Florida Airlines	ZO	(800) FAST-JET
Hawaiin	HA	(800) 367-5320
MGM Grand Air	MG	(800) 933-2646
Midway Airlines	ML	(800) 621-5700
Midwest Express	YX	(800) 452-2022
New England Airlines	EJ	(800) 243-2460

continued...

Northwest	NW	(800) 225-2525
Pan American	PA	(800) 221-1111
Southwest (outside Texas)	WN	(800) 531-5601
TWA	TW	(800) 221-2000
		(800) 892-4141 (int'l)
US Air	US	(800) 428-4322
United Airlines	UA	(800) 241-6522
		(800) 631-1500

Foreign Airlines

Aer Lingus	EI	(800) 223-6537
Aerolineas Argentina	AR	(800) 333-0276
Aeromexico	AM	(800) AEROMEX
AeroPeru	PL	(800) 255-7378
Air Canada	AC	(800) 4-CANADA
Air France	AF	(800) 237-2747
Air India	AI	(800) 223-7776
Air Jamaica	JM	(800) 523-5585
Air Paraguay	PZ	(800) 677-7771
Alitalia	AZ	(800) 223-5730
All Nipon Airways	NA	(800) 235-9262
Ansett Airlines	AN	(800) 366-1300
Avianca	AV	(800) 327-9899
British Airways	BA	(800) AIRWAYS
BWIA	BW	(800) 327-7401
Canadian Airlines	CP	(800) 426-7000
Cathay Pacific	CA	(800) 233-2742

Cayman Airways	KX	(800) 422-9626
China Airlines	CI	(800) 227-5118
Ecuatoriana Airlines	EU	(800) 328-2367
Egypt Air	MS	(800) 334-6787
El Al	LY	(800) 223-6700
Finnair	AY	(800) 950-5000
Iberia	IB	(800) 772-4642
Icelandair	FI	(800) 223-5500
Japan Air Lines	JL	(800) 525-3663
KLM	KL	(800) 525-3663
Korean	KE	(800) 421-8200
Lan Chile	LA	(800) 735-5526
Lacsa	LR	(800) 522-7201
Lot Polish Airlines		(800) 223-0593
Lufthansa	LH	(800) 645-3880
Malaysia	MG	(800) 421-8641
Mexicana	MX	(800) 531-7921
Olympic Airways	OA	(800) 223-1226
Pakistani Airlines	PK	(800) 221-2552
Phillipine Airlines	PR	(800) 1-FLYPAL
Qantas Airways	QF	(800) 227-4500
Royal Jordanian	RJ	(800) 223-0470
SAS	SK	(800) 221-2350
Sabena Belgian Airlines	SN	(800) 955-2000

continued...

Singapore Airlines	SQ	(800) 742-3333
Skywest	OO	(800) 453-9417
South African Airways	SA	(800) 722-9675
Swissair	SR	(800) 221-4750
TAP	TP	(800) 221-7370
Taca International	TA	(800) 535-8780
Thai Airways	TG	(800) 426-5204
Trans World Airlines	TW	(800) 438-2929
		(800) 221-2000
Varig Brazilian	RG	(800) GO-VARIG
Yugoslav Airlines	JU	(800) 752-6528

APPENDIX
II
METHODS TO SAVE MONEY
AND FLY FREE

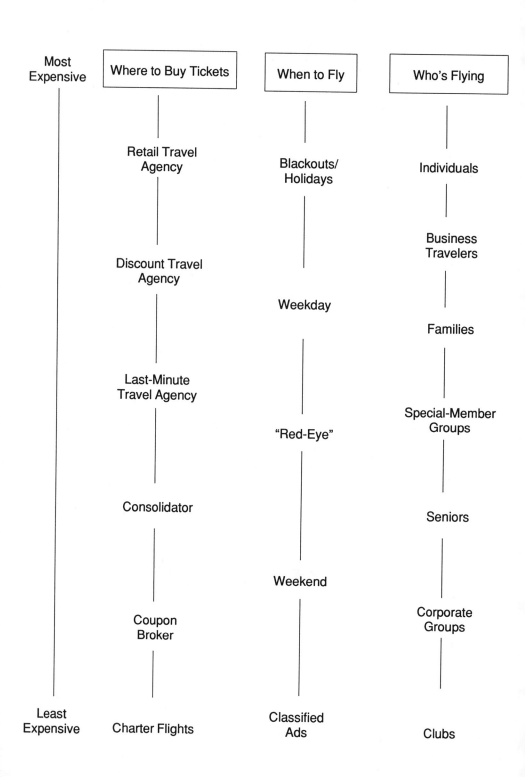

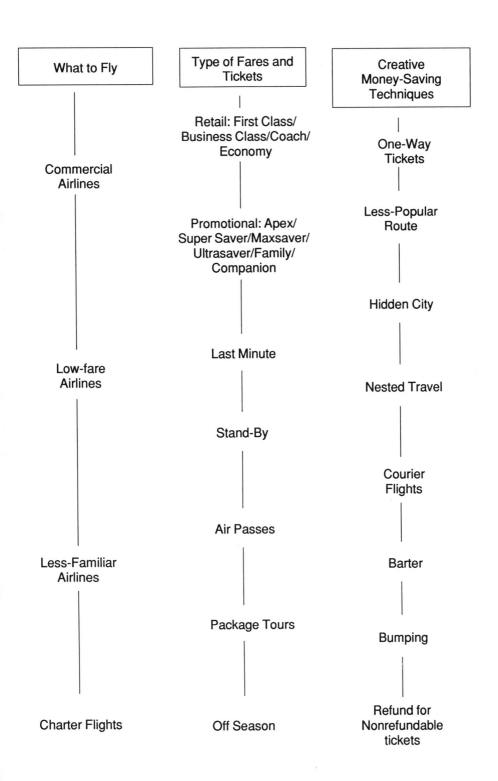

What to Fly	Type of Fares and Tickets	Creative Money-Saving Techniques
Commercial Airlines	Retail: First Class/ Business Class/Coach/ Economy	One-Way Tickets
	Promotional: Apex/ Super Saver/Maxsaver/ Ultrasaver/Family/ Companion	Less-Popular Route
		Hidden City
Low-fare Airlines	Last Minute	
	Stand-By	Nested Travel
	Air Passes	Courier Flights
Less-Familiar Airlines		Barter
	Package Tours	Bumping
Charter Flights	Off Season	Refund for Nonrefundable tickets

APPENDIX
III
WHO TO CALL IF
YOU HAVE A PROBLEM

APPENDIX III
WHO TO CALL IF YOU
HAVE A PROBLEM

Over 12,000 passengers complain to the United States airlines each year. Their problems and difficulties run the gamut from being bumped from overbooked flights, to onboard safety infractions, to poor service and overcooked meals. The following are some important organizations associated with the travel industry who work to inform, help and support individual travelers:

AMERICAN SOCIETY OF TRAVEL AGENTS. 1101 King St., Alexandria, VA 22314, (703) 739-2782. ASTA is the largest trade group for travel agencies. They also operate a Consumer Affairs Department to mediate disputes between consumers, member agencies and their suppliers. There is also a Tour Protection Plan that guarantees pre-payment on a tour booked by a member agency if a tour operator fails.

U.S. DEPARTMENT OF TRANSPORTATION, OFFICE OF CONSUMER AFFAIRS, (202) 366-2220. You can check with them if you are unsure of a travel agency you are buying from. They will advise you whether any complaints have been filed against the agency. Travelers wishing to file complaints about airline service with the Office of Consumer Affairs may do so, in addition to a written complaint to the airline's president and its consumer affairs department.

FEDERAL AVIATION ADMINISTRATION. (800) 322-7873. This is the FAA's consumer hotline for questions regarding air safety or reporting unusual flight conditions.

UNITED STATES TOUR OPERATOR ASSOCIATION. 211 E. 51st St., Suite 12B, New York, NY 10022, (212) 944-5727. The USTOA also mediates complaints between consumers and member tour companies. Members include more than 40 of the country's largest wholesale tour operators.

U.S. STATE DEPARTMENT CITIZEN EMERGENCY CENTER. (202) 647-5225. Their hotline will update travelers on the latest travel advisories for United States citizens planning travel abroad. With the recent Middle East crisis and other areas of political unrest, there is no shortage of hot spots where travel for Americans is not advised.

TRAVEL ASSISTANCE INTERNATIONAL. (800) 821-2828. This organization provides a free consumer guide with information on financial and medical services abroad.

U.S. DEPARTMENT OF TRANSPORTATION, OFFICE OF CONSUMER AFFAIRS. 400 7th Street, S.W. Rm. 10405, Washington, D.C. 20590, (202) 366-2220. In addition to accepting and reporting complaints, DOT publishes a monthly "Air Travel Consumer Report," which tracks information and ranks the airlines on-time performances for departing and arriving.

AVIATION CONSUMER ACTION PROJECT. P.O. Box 19029, Washington, D.C. 20036, (202) 293-9142. This non-profit group, set up by Ralph Nader 20 years ago, acts as a watchdog for the rights of traveling passengers aiding them in complaints against the airlines, to the point of representing citizens in litigation. Contact them if you have experienced difficulties with baggage, bumping, service and meals, and unusual delays, or safety violation. For $2 the ACAP will send you their detailed booklet, *Facts and Advice for Airline Passengers*.

FREE TO ALL PURCHASERS OF "THE MORE FOR YOUR MONEY GUIDES"

New and exciting free and deeply discounted offers are always being initiated and old ones rediscovered. To keep you informed and up-to-date on all the latest and best free offers and methods that you can take advantage of, we are offering all purchasers of our *More For Your Money Guides* a free issue of our "Best Things in Life for Free" newsletter.

Don't miss out on the newest and most innovative free opportunities available to you. Just send a self-addressed, stamped envelope to:

"Best Things in Life for Free"
P.O. Box 6661
Malibu, CA 90265

Some of the best things in life can be free! We are dedicated to providing the most fantastic, undiscovered and overloaded ideas and methods to obtain free goods, products and services for you and your family, and to alert you to the many opportunities to live, travel and enjoy life with little or no money. And, best of all, this information is free to our readers, just for asking.

Also perhaps you've also already had success with ideas of your own that have worked for you, that I haven't included in this book. If so, I would very much like to hear from you. Not only will sharing your ideas and successes be beneficial to others, but we will also pay $100 to the first person sending in an idea or method that we use in subsequent editions of our books, and $50 if it is used in our newsletter.

Additional *More For Your Money Guides* Available From Probus Publishing

Free Food ... and More, Linda Bowman,
   Order #220, $9.95

How to Go to College for Free, Linda Bowman,
   Order #219, $9.95

Freebies (and More) for Folks Over 50, Linda Bowman,
   Order #218, $9.95

Forthcoming Titles

Free Stuff for Your Pet, Linda Bowman,
   Order #271, $9.95

Free Stuff for Kids and Parents Too!, Linda Bowman,
   Order #272, $9.95

USE ORDER FORM ON NEXT PAGE TO ORDER!

ORDER FORM

Quantity	Order #	Title	Price

Payment: MasterCard/Visa/American Express accepted. When ordering by credit card your account will not be billed until the book is shipped. You may also reserve your order by phone or by mailing this order form. When ordering by check or money order, you will be invoiced upon publication. Upon receipt of your payment, the book will be shipped. Please add $3.50 for postage and handling for the first book and $1.00 for each additional copy.

Subtotal	
IL residents add 7% tax	
Shipping and Handling	
Total	

Credit Card # _____

Expiration Date _____

Name _____

Address _____

City, State, Zip _____

Telephone _____

Signature _____

Mail Orders to:

PROBUS PUBLISHING COMPANY
1925 N. Clybourn Avenue
Chicago, IL 60614

or Call:

1-800 PROBUS-1